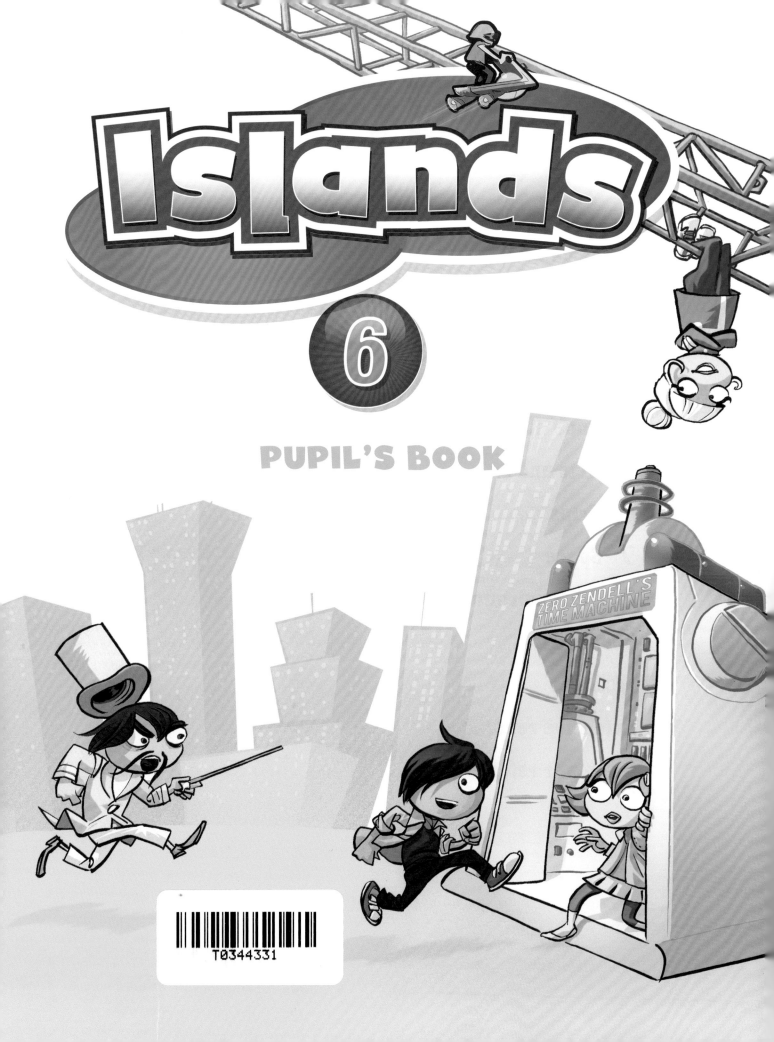

Islands

6

PUPIL'S BOOK

ZERO ZENDELL'S TIME MACHINE

T0344331

Contents

Scope and sequence

Welcome

Grammar	Vocabulary	Additional language
Does it look good? Yes, it does. / No, it doesn't. What does it (look) like? It looks (good). / It looks (like) (a cake). You are a …, aren't you? He is a …, isn't he? She is a …, isn't she?	look, smell, taste, sound, feel singer, secretary, gardener, receptionist, actor, tour guide, chemist See you! See you later/tonight/tomorrow/next week! See you in two days/half an hour! See you on Tuesday!	

1 Adventure camp

Grammar	Vocabulary	Additional language
Tom is good at (sports). I like (hiking), but I don't like (sailing). I love (fishing) and (camping).	**Camping equipment:** sleeping bag, tent, rucksack, pegs, compass, torch, campsite, fire	**CLIL:** Science (Deforestation) **Wider World:** Camping around the world **Values:** Safety first! Think about safety when you go camping. **Phonics & Spelling:** Inflectional endings -ed/-ing
We're pitching the tent. We're putting in the pegs. I can pitch a tent but I can't read a compass. I'm cold so I'm lighting a fire.	**Camping activities:** pitch the tent, take down the tent, put in the pegs, lay out the bed, cover our heads, light a fire, keep out the rain, read a compass	
	CLIL: river, sea, before, after, deforestation	

2 Wildlife park

Grammar	Vocabulary	Additional language
How (heavy) is it? It's 800 kilogrammes. How (tall) is it? It's five metres tall. The (giraffe) is (taller) than the (rhino). The (giraffe) is the (tallest).	**Wild animals:** rhino, cheetah, panther, lemur, camel, whale, seal, otter, turtle, tiger	**CLIL:** Science (Fossils) **Wider World:** City animals **Values:** Think before you act! Think carefully before making important decisions. **Phonics & Spelling:** Comparative and superlative endings -er and -est
Are (otters) more dangerous than (snakes)? Yes, they are. / No, they aren't. Were the (trees) taller than the (houses)? Yes, they were. / No, they weren't. Which is the (heaviest)? The (hippo) is the (heaviest).	**Superlative adjectives:** tallest, longest, shortest, biggest, smallest, heaviest, lightest, fastest, slowest	
Simple passive It is found … Information can be seen …	**CLIL:** fossils, dinosaur, octopus, swan	

3 Where we live

Grammar	Vocabulary	Additional language
How do you get to the (swimming pool)? (Turn left) at the (corner), then go (straight ahead). The (swimming pool) is in the (sports centre), at the end of the (building). near / between / next to / behind / straight ahead / at the end of / in front of If you walk to the park, you will find the shop at the end of the street.	Places (1): shopping centre, post office, cinema, chemist, newsagent, college, circus, factory, theatre Places (2): university, airport, bookshop, fire station, police station, railway station, bus stop, guest house, stadium, underground CLIL: left, right, urban, rural, population, east, west, north, south	CLIL: Maths (Graphing population) Wider World: Our homes Values: Learn to be flexible! It's often frustrating to have to do what you don't want to do. Phonics & Spelling: Suffixes -ful and -ly

4 Good and bad days

Grammar	Vocabulary	Additional language
I cooked a stew. He dropped the plate. She paddled very fast. We fell in the lake. We ate an omelette. What happened? I didn't pass my test because I didn't revise. It made me sad! I played tennis with my friends because it didn't rain. It made me happy! *Past continuous* She/He was eating. They were drinking.	International food: curry, fish and chips, paella, spaghetti, omelette, dumplings, stew, sushi, rice and beans Verbs and objects: pack my bag, miss the bus, pass a test, open a lunchbox, remember my juice, drop the ball CLIL: sedentary, physical activity, vitamins, minerals, nutrients	CLIL: Social sciences (Healthy habits) Wider World: Food traditions Values: Be positive about your day. Don't worry. Be happy! Phonics & Spelling: Review simple past -ed: /t/ /d/ /id/

5 Arts and entertainment

Grammar	Vocabulary	Additional language
I saw the film by myself. You wrote it by yourself, didn't you? He made it by himself, didn't he? She didn't watch the film by herself, did she? They didn't draw it by themselves, did they? Have you ever played the saxophone? Yes, I've played it since I was seven. Have you heard that song yet? Yes, I've just heard it on the radio. How long have you been at the concert? I've been here for 2 hours. *Past simple interrupting past continuous action:* I was … *(+ing)*, when I *(-ed)* … They were … *(+ing)*, when they *(-ed)* … I was reading a book when she phoned.	Film genres: thriller, comedy, sci-fi, romance, musical, cartoon Musical instruments: cello, harmonica, saxophone, triangle, drums, clarinet, harp, tambourine CLIL: rock, blues, country, pop, jazz	CLIL: Music (Types of music) Wider World: World instruments Values: Learn to be self-sufficient! You can always do some things by yourself. Phonics & Spelling: Adding prefixes

6 Trips

Grammar	Vocabulary	Additional language
What will you do tomorrow? First, I'll go to the castle. Then, I'll go to the museum. Last, I'll go to the water park! Shall we (go on the big wheel)? I'm not sure. What else could we do? We could (go on the rollercoaster). I may *(+verb)* = *possibility* I might *(+verb)* = *less possibility* May I … *(+verb)*? = *permission*	**Tourist attractions:** museum, aquarium, amusement park, palace, water park, castle, National Park **Amusement park attractions:** go on the big wheel, go on the dodgems, play mini-golf, go on the carousel, go on the boating lake, go on the rollercoaster, go on the pirate ship, go on the water slide **CLIL:** drought, fog, storm, rain, snow	**CLIL:** Science (Weather) **Wider World:** Our holidays **Values:** Plan, but be flexible! Planning helps you do more things. **Phonics & Spelling:** Question tags and intonation

7 Space

Grammar	Vocabulary	Additional language
We should go outside tonight to see the stars. We'd better get ready. We need to bring the telescope. It's cold. We ought to wear our jackets! Which planet is more interesting? The red planet is more interesting than the blue planet. Which planet is the most interesting? The red planet is the most interesting. Which telescope is less complicated? The small telescope is less complicated than the big telescope. Which telescope is the least complicated? The small telescope is the least complicated. *Reported Speech* He/she says he/she … *(present simple)* They say they … *(present simple)*	**Space:** astronaut, planet, comet, telescope, alien, spaceship, satellite, rocket, boosters, space station **Adjectives:** complicated, amazing, frightening, intelligent, brilliant, important, interesting, expensive, horrible **CLIL:** concave, convex, distorted image, curved mirror, reflect	**CLIL:** Science (Distorting mirrors) **Wider World:** Space facts **Values:** Use your imagination when you are trying to solve a problem. **Phonics & Spelling:** sm-, st-, sk-, sp-, sc- versus es

8 The environment

Grammar	Vocabulary	Additional language
I'm going to recycle paper because we need to protect our environment. He's/She's going to recycle bottles. We're/They're going to collect the rubbish. Are you going to help? Yes, I am. / No, I'm not. What can you do to help? I can use public transport. If you reuse plastic bags, you'll reduce waste.	**Ways to help the environment:** recycle paper, recycle bottles, collect rubbish, reuse plastic bags, turn off the lights, use public transport **Environmentally friendly outcomes:** save trees, save resources, keep the planet clean, reduce waste, conserve energy, reduce pollution **CLIL:** allergies, ambulance, pollution, sneezing	**CLIL:** Social sciences (Allergies) **Wider World:** What are we doing to our planet? **Values:** Save our planet. Learn to save energy and keep the planet clean! **Phonics & Spelling:** Suffixes -tion/sion

Goodbye

Revision		

Festivals

Bonfire Night: bonfire night, fireworks, gunpowder, plot, Houses of Parliament, sparklers

Christmas crackers: snap! toilet roll, crossed arms

Boxing Day: Bank holiday

Easter eggs: hard-boiled, food colouring, vinegar, stickers, pattern, silver

Wimbledon: championship, tickets, game-set-match!

Welcome

Today ...

1:02 **Listen and read. What are Zero Zendell's plans?**

Year 2210

2 **Listen and read. Then answer.**

2 This is Serena. Serena is outside all the time and knows a lot. She's good at running and jumping. She can climb walls, too!

Serena

1 This is Zero Zendell. He always wears a top hat and has got a long moustache. He has got the only animals on Future Island in his zoo. But the people are bored with seeing the same animals. Zero Zendell has a plan to make his zoo more popular, but it's illegal and dangerous!

Zero Zendell

Present day

3 This is Marta who lives with her parents in a nature reserve. She's brave but sometimes gets into arguments quickly. She goes everywhere with her chimpanzee, Champ.

Marta

4 This is Chris. Chris has got long dark hair. He's a clever boy but he's not so active—not like Marta. But they're good friends. He likes to think carefully about things, too. Chris doesn't like getting wet or dirty.

Chris

5 This is Champ, the chimpanzee. Wild dogs were trying to attack him so Marta's dad rescued him. Now Marta looks after Champ. Champ is always very friendly and he's happy with his new life in the nature reserve.

Champ

a What does Zero Zendell do on Future Island?

b What is Zero Zendell's problem?

c What is Serena good at?

d What unusual thing can Serena do?

3 **Listen and repeat.**

1 look **2** smell
3 taste **4** sound
5 feel

LOOK!

Does it **look** good?	Yes, it does. / No, it doesn't.
What does it **look like**?	It **looks** good.
	It **looks like** a cake.

4 **Listen and point.**

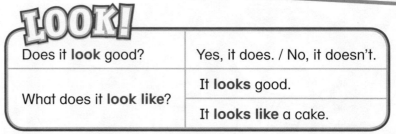

a   b   c   d

LOOK!

He/She is …, isn't he/she?

He/She isn't …, is he/she?

They/You are …, aren't they/you?

They/You aren't …, are they/you?

5 **Read and find the question tag in the box.**

isn't he?   are they?   isn't she?   is he?   isn't he?

1   Champ is very friendly.

3   Serena is good at climbing walls.

2   He isn't sad with his new family.

4   People aren't having fun at the zoo.

5   Zero Zendell is thinking about doing something illegal.

6 **Read and say. Use a question tag at the end.**

a   The visitor numbers aren't going up,

b   Zero Zendell is very strange,

c   Champ is very nice,

d   The zoo is losing money,

7 **Ask and answer.**

a   You are a …, aren't you?

b   We are learning …, aren't we?

c   Our parents are …, aren't they?

d   We … on Future Island, are we?

You are 13 years old, aren't you?

8 🔘 1:07 **Listen and repeat.**

1 singer

2 secretary

3 gardener

4 hairdresser

5 receptionist

6 tour guide

7 chemist

9 **Read and say. What do these people do on Future Island?**

1 I can show you Future Island. It looks very different here. I can take you to see the zoo.

2 My chemicals look strange, but I can do great experiments.

3 Do you like spiky hair? Her hairstyles look very nice.

4 His voice sounds nice. He's very good at singing!

5 My garden looks beautiful. Do you need help with yours?

6 Her office looks perfect. She organises everything.

7 She works at reception. She looks very friendly!

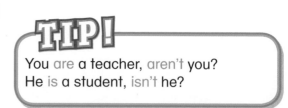

TIP!

You are a teacher, aren't you?
He is a student, isn't he?

10 🔘 **Listen and repeat.**

1 See you! **2** See you soon!

3 See you later! **4** See you tomorrow!

5 See you next week! **6** See you tonight!

7 See you in two days! **8** See you in half an hour!

9 See you on Tuesday!

11 **Read. What do you say?**

See you later!

See you tonight!

1 It's 5 o'clock. You're meeting your friend again at 7 o'clock.

2 It's time to go home. You're coming back tomorrow.

3 It's Monday. You're meeting your friend again on Wednesday.

4 You are talking to a neighbour at the park. It's time to go.

5 You see your teacher in the playground. You've got a lesson with her later.

6 Today is Friday. You're meeting your uncle on Monday.

7 It's the afternoon. You're meeting a friend that same night.

8 It's 4 o'clock. You're meeting your friend again at half past 4.

9 Today is Sunday. You're meeting your friend again in 2 days.

1 Adventure camp

1 🔘 1:10 **Listen and read. Who is Tom's sister?**

Adventure Camp!
Remember to bring these things:
tent   sleeping bag   pegs   compass   rucksack   torch
Please send in information about yourself by 20th May.
See you there!

Hannah: Hi, there. I'm Hannah. What are your names?
Maria: I'm Maria.
Felipe: And I'm Felipe.
Tom: I'm Tom and this is my sister ...
Flo: I'm Flo.
Hannah: Great, let's see ... Maria, yes ... Felipe, yes ... Tom, yes ... Flo ... yes ... Welcome to the camp, guys!

2 🔘 1:11 **Listen and repeat.**

1
sleeping bag

3
rucksack

4
pegs

6
torch

2
tent

5
compass

7
campsite

8
fire

3 Ask and answer: What do you need to go camping?
You need...

4 🔊 *1:13* **Listen and read. Then say *True* or *False*.**

1 This is Tom. He's fourteen and he's British. He loves playing basketball and football. He can cook and swim, but he can't surf. He has one sister, Flo. She's twelve and she's very funny.

2 Her name's Maria and she's thirteen. She's from Mexico. She likes dancing but she's not very good at singing! She has two sisters. They're eight and ten and she loves playing with them.

3 This is Flo and she's twelve. She's from the United Kingdom. She's good at swimming. She loves talking to her friends. She has one brother. He's fourteen and he's very good at sports. He's very clever, too.

4 This is Felipe. He's from Spain. He's thirteen. He loves playing video games and he likes Science and Maths. He has three brothers and they love video games, too. They always have competitions.

1 Tom and Flo are from the same country.

2 Felipe and Maria are fourteen years old.

3 Flo is one year younger than Maria.

4 Tom, Maria, Flo and Felipe have the same hobbies.

LOOK!

Tom is **good at** sports.

I **like** hiking, but I **don't like** sailing.

I **love** fishing and camping.

5 **Ask and answer.**

1 Where are Tom and Flo from?
2 What does Tom love doing?
3 How old are Maria's sisters?
4 What subjects does Felipe like?

6 **Imagine you are Tom, Maria, Flo, or Felipe. Ask and answer.**

1 How old are you?
2 Where are you from?
3 What do you like doing?
4 What are you good at?
5 Have you got any brothers or sisters?

7 **1:15** Listen and repeat.

1  pitch the tent

2  take down the tent

3  put in the pegs

4  lay out the bed

5  cover our heads

6  light a fire

7  keep out the rain

8 read a compass

8 **1:16** Listen to the song. Which words are missing? **SONG**

Scouts from all around the world, from Spain to Italy,
We're travelling together, from the … to the sea.
We walk for miles and learn every day.
We read a … and find our way.
CHORUS:
Oh, we are adventure scouts, here is our song.
With adventure and new friends, you can't go wrong.
You can't go wrong.
At the end of the day, we're back to camp again.
We're pitching our tents, they keep out the …
We're putting in the pegs and laying out our beds.
We're sleeping in sleeping bags that cover our heads!
Chorus
All this adventure is making us fit and strong.
We're cooking our … which
doesn't take too long.
We're eating our dinner and then we're so tired.
We're sleeping in … all around the fire!
Chorus

9 **1:17** Listen again. Which activities are not in the song?

1 reading a compass
3 running a race
5 putting in the pegs

2 pitching a tent
4 eating breakfast
6 playing in a band

10 **Listen and point. Then match.**

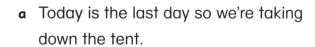

1

a Today is the last day so we're taking down the tent.

2

b I'm at the campsite and I'm pitching the tent.

3

c I'm lost, but I can read a compass.

4

d I'm putting in the pegs.

5

e I want to cook dinner so I'm lighting a fire.

6

f It's raining so we're covering our heads.

7

g It's evening now so I'm laying out the bed.

LOOK!

I **can** pitch a tent, **but** I **can't** read a compass.

I'm cold **so** I'm lighting a fire.

11 **Listen and match. Then say.**

1

2

3

4

a

b

He's pitching the tent.

c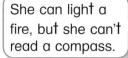

d

e

f

g

She can light a fire, but she can't read a compass.

h

12 Look at the pictures. Tell the story.

13 🔘 1:22 Listen and read. Why does Chris say he knows that place? Then act out.

> **Inflectional endings –ed and –ing**
>
> We add **–ed** and **–ing** to verb forms: work → work**ed** or work**ing**.
> • When a verb ends in **–e**, we only add **–d,** and **–ing** makes the final **e** disappear:
> • vote → vot**ed**, vot**ing**.
> • When a verb ends in stressed/short vowel + one consonant (except w or y), we double the consonant:
>   stop → sto**pped**, sto**pping**.
> • When a verb ends in consonant + **-y**, we change **-y** to **-i** and add **–ed**:
>   study → stud**ied**, stud**ying**.

14 **Listen and repeat.**

1 chat → cha**tt**ed, cha**tt**ing
2 plan → pla**nn**ed, pla**nn**ing
3 shop → sho**pp**ed, sho**pp**ing
4 stop → sto**pp**ed, sto**pp**ing
5 hop → ho**pp**ed, ho**pp**ing

-ed -ing

15 **Read and blend the words with a partner.**

1 beat**ing** / be**tt**ing
2 catch**ing** / cu**tt**ing
3 rain**ing** / ru**nn**ing
4 pack**ing** / pla**nn**ing
5 book**ing** / pu**tt**ing
6 hop**ing** / ho**pp**ing

16 **Read and practise.**

chat → I **chatted** with my friends at school.
I was **chatting** with them when the bell rang.

plan → Yesterday, we **planned** our holidays.
The teacher is **planning** our next lesson.

stop → I **stopped** learning Spanish last year.
She was **stopping** when the traffic light changed.

hop → She **hopped** in the sports lesson.
She is very good at **hopping**.

17 **Listen and repeat.**

SOUNDS FUN!

I can dive and swim in the sea.
But he's good at swim**ming** and likes eat**ing** me!

18 **Read and find the words below in the text. What is the rainforest like before deforestation?**

after   before   deforestation   rivers   seas

Deforestation

before

A rainforest is a dense jungle where it rains a lot. It's a hot and humid place. Brazil has got one of the most important rainforests in the world – The Amazon.

The rainforest is home to some amazing plants and animals. 30 million species of plants and animals live there! The rainforest has got the perfect conditions for these animals to live in.

Chocolate, pineapples and sugar are some things that come from rainforests.

deforestation

Deforestation is the process of clearing forests on Earth. It happens for many reasons, for example, to use the land to grow food or to sell the wood to make paper and other products. Often people make more money selling the trees than conserving the rainforest.

after

Rainforest areas about as big as a football field disappear every minute.

Deforestation can cause drought: a lack of water. This can cause the extinction of plant and animal species in the rainforest and other habitats like rivers or seas.

Deforestation is also a key factor in climate change.

What's a rainforest?

It's …

19 **Ask and answer.**

1 What is a rainforest?
2 What is deforestation?
3 What does a rainforest look like before deforestation?
4 What does a rainforest look like after deforestation?

20 **Think about forests in your country. Then talk with your partner.**

Before deforestation it was …

After deforestation it is …

1 Are there any forests where you live?
2 Are they suffering any kind of deforestation?
3 What can we do to solve this problem?

Wider world
Camping around the world

21 **Read. Match the words in blue to the photos.**

1

The Lake District is a great place for camping. It's the largest National Park in the UK. I usually visit the Lake District in the spring with my family. I love riding my bike on the paths in the mountains. Mountain biking can be difficult but it's very exciting. When we are not at the campsite, my dad also likes sailing. There are many different types of fish in the lakes. The mountains and the grassy valleys here are lovely!

Melissa, 12, United Kingdom

2

Camping in Thailand is great fun. My favourite place is a National Park called Khao Sam Roi Yot. Khao Sam Roi Yot means the mountain with 300 peaks. The mountains are very difficult to climb. There are a lot of things to see around the park. I like watching the lovely birds and other wild animals like deer and squirrels. There are a lot of interesting caves, too. Thailand is an exciting place!

Alak, 12, Thailand

3

Vulcano is a small volcanic island in Italy. I like camping there in the summer with my grandparents. We sleep in a big tent in the forest. During the day, my grandad rides a motorbike around the island.
I like hiking to the top of the volcano. My granny likes walking on the black sandy beaches near the sea. There is special mud in Vulcano that is very good for your skin. Some people like putting the mud on their bodies. I love visiting Vulcano!

Luca, 11, Italy

22 **Ask and answer.**

What can you see both in Khao Sam Roi Yot and the Lake District?

What does Alak like watching?

Why does Luca like visiting Vulcano?

Which of these places would you like to visit?

23 **Where can you go camping in your country? Tell a partner.**

PORTFOLIO

Think and talk.

Describe an ideal camping trip.

HAVE FUN!

● I'm good at …   ● I love …

○ I like …, but I don't like ….   ● I can …, but I can't ….

I'm good at swimming.

START

1

2 You didn't bring the pegs. Throw a 3 to continue.

3

4 It's good weather. Move 1 space.

5

6 You're good at pitching the tent. Move 2 spaces.

7

8

9 It starts raining before you finish pitching the tent. Miss a turn.

10

11 It's dark but you have a torch and new batteries. Take another turn.

12

13 You get wood for the fire but it's wet! Miss a turn.

14

15 You find new wood for the fire and cook dinner. Move 2 spaces.

16

17

18 You didn't bring a sleeping bag. Throw a 6 to continue.

19

FINISH

AB p.1

Pictur Diction

25 **Read and choose the right word.**

1 He's very good at *(reading / use / buy)* a compass.

2 We're putting in the *(rucksack / pegs / torch)* for our tent.

3 Where *(was / does / do)* he like going?

4 Come on! We need to pitch the tent *(before / after / now)* the rain comes.

26 **Read and say. What is it?**

1 An object for finding the way. It has a needle that points north.

2 A light that works with batteries.

3 A large bag to carry things on your back.

4 Something that makes smoke. It can also produce heat.

27 **Read and ask.**

Read to B:

Katy likes travelling to other countries. Her family loves camping. She likes walking in the forest. She's very good at reading her compass. She never gets lost.

Ask B:

1 What does Katy like?

2 What is she good at?

3 Why doesn't she get lost?

Read to A:

Michael doesn't like camping. His family loves going to the mountains at the weekends. He's very good at climbing high mountains. He always brings some water in his rucksack in case he gets thirsty.

Ask A:

1 What does Michael like?

2 What is he good at?

3 Why does he always bring some water in his rucksack?

1 🔊 1:27 **Listen and read. Where was Flo?**

There you all are! Where **were** you?

We were with the cheetahs. They were **really** fast!

I was with the snakes. They were **really** long!

I was with the elephant.

Cool! How big was it?

Really big! And it was **really** naughty!

2 🔊 1:28 **Listen and repeat.**

| 1 | 2 | 3 | 4 | 5 |

 rhino   cheetah    panther    lemur    camel

 whale   seal    otter   turtle    tiger

3 **Ask and answer.**

How many of these animals live on land?

How many of these animals live in the water?

TIP!
1600 = one thousand, six hundred
3250 = three thousand, two hundred and fifty

4 🔊 1:30 **Look and listen. Which animal is Tom describing?**

Name: Roddy
How heavy? 1,600 kilogrammes
How tall?   two metres
How long?   three metres
How fast?   fast!

Name: Geri
How heavy? 800 kilogrammes
How tall?   five metres
How long?   three metres
How fast?   fast!

5 **Look and ask questions.**

1 tall / the giraffe?
2 heavy / the rhino?
3 fast / the rhino?
4 long / the giraffe?
5 tall / the rhino?
6 heavy / the giraffe?

LOOK!

How heavy is it?	It's 800 kilogrammes.
How tall is it?	It's five metres tall.
The giraffe is **taller than** the rhino.	

> How tall is the giraffe?

> It's five metres tall.

6 **Look. Then ask and answer. What animal is it?**

3.5 metres

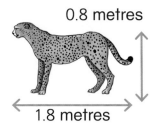

0.8 metres

1.2 metres

1.8 metres

2.5 metres

7 metres

> How tall is it?

> It's 3.5 metres tall.

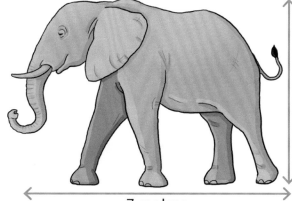

7 **1:32** **Listen and repeat.**

① tallest
② longest
③ shortest
④ biggest
⑤ smallest
⑥ heaviest
⑦ lightest
⑧ fastest
⑨ slowest

8 **1:33** **Listen to the song.** SONG

9 **Look at the table. Which animals are in the song?**

Take me to a place where the days are longer,
Where I can be with the animals, wild and free.
Take me to a place where the trees are taller
Than the houses and the buildings in the big city.

In the sea there are seals, smaller than otters.
There are blue whales, longer than my street.
Can you see the turtles, swimming in the blue water?
They're bigger than my pet fish but they've got feet!

Chorus

In the jungle there are tigers, faster than taxis.
There are panthers, darker than the night.
I want to see the lemurs, sitting in the trees.
I really love wild animals, orange, black or white!

Habitat	Sea	Jungle
Animals	whales fish turtles otters seals octopuses	tigers panthers lemurs gorillas cheetahs

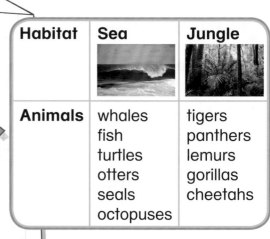

LOOK!

Are otters **more dangerous than** snakes?	No, they aren't.
Were the trees **taller than** the houses?	Yes, they were.
Which is **the heaviest**?	The hippo is **the heaviest**.

10 **Look and listen. Then ask and answer.**

1 Are rhinos heavier than seals?   Which animal is the heaviest?
2 Are otters faster than panthers?   Which animal is the fastest?
3 Are snakes louder than lemurs?   Which animal is the loudest?
4 Are turtles longer than ants?   Which animal is the longest?

11 Read and say.

> Giraffes are the tallest. Tigers are taller than otters.

1 giraffes / otters / tigers   (tall)   2 hippos / lemurs / turtles   (slow)

3 elephants / turtles / hippos   (heavy)   4 panthers / giraffes / cheetahs (fast)

12 Look at the table. Ask and answer.

> Which animal …?

Life span

Animal	In the zoo	In the wild
rhino	35 years	30 years
lemur	27 years	15 years
panda	20 years	10 years

1 Which animal has got the shortest life?
2 Which animal has got the longest life?
3 Where do these animals live a longer life? Why?
4 Where do these animals live a shorter life? Why?

13 Look at the pictures. Tell the story.

14 1:35 Listen and find out. Why does Serena think that Marta and Chris are rich? Then act out.

1

You're funny! Where are you from?

WE'RE not funny! YOU are!

We're lost. And we can't find our chimpanzee.

2

Chimpanzee?!! WOW! Are you rich?

No, we aren't. We were in this time machine ...

3

Hmm. They say Zero Zendell's got a time machine. And he wants animals at **any** price.

Do you think Champ is valuable?!!

Of **course**!

4

This park is **very** small.

Park? It's a **museum**! And you **can't** sit on the grass! The guards ...

5

RUN!! They're coming ...

6

PHEW!! That was close! Thanks Serena.

We're **lost**. We **can't** go home. And we **can't** find **Champ**.

Don't worry, I'm your friend and I want to help you.

VALUES

Think before you act! Think carefully before making important decisions.

HOME-SCHOOL LINK

Tell your family about an important decision you made today.

 PARENT

> **Comparative and superlative endings** –er and –est.
>
> We add –er and –est to one- or two-syllable adjectives.
> If it ends in …
> • –e, we only add –r and –st: late → later, latest.
> • one vowel + one consonant, we double the consonant except w: big → bigger, biggest.
> • a consonant + -y, we change –y to –i and add –er or –est: heavy → heavier, heaviest.

15 **Listen and repeat.**

-er   -est

16 **Listen, point and say.**

1	2	3	4
-er / -est	-e + r / -e + st	1 vowel + 1 consonant	-ier / -iest

1 tall → taller, tallest
3 short → shorter, shortest
5 small → smaller, smallest
7 light → lighter, lightest
9 slow → slower, slowest

2 long → longer, longest
4 big → bigger, biggest
6 heavy → heavier, heaviest
8 fast → faster, fastest
10 late → later, latest

17 **Read and blend the words with a partner.**

1 The camel is taller than the panther.
3 The whale is the biggest.
5 The turtle is friendlier than the rhino.

2 The rhino is fatter than the cheetah.
4 The lemur looks the happiest!

18  **Listen and repeat.**

SOUNDS FUN!

Of these three friends …
The cheetah is the fastest.
The whale is the biggest and heaviest.
And the otter is the smallest and the lightest!

19 **Read and find the words below in the text. Then look and say. How are a fossil and a shell similar/different?**

dinosaur   fossils   swan   octopus

Fossils

Dinosaurs lived a long time ago but they are all extinct now. We know about them because palaeontologists study their fossils. Palaeontology is the scientific study of past life by analysing animal and plant fossils. A lot of information can be seen by palaeontologists when a fossil is found. They can tell if the animal had fur or not, if it could fly or not and many other details by studying the shape and the structure of the fossil. The shape of the wing of a flying dinosaur was not so different to that of the swan or any other bird today. There are fossils of big animals (dinosaurs, elephants etc.) and fossils of very small animals such as insects (butterflies, ants etc.) Marine fossils are also found under the sea by marine archaeologists. Scientists can find out about the life history of the octopus by studying fossils.

20 **Ask and answer.**

1   How do we know what dinosaurs were like?

2   What kind of information can be found in a fossil?

3   What kinds of fossils are there?

21 **Read. Then ask and answer.**

1   Have you ever seen a fossil?
2   What kind of fossil was it?
3   Where did you find it?
4   What information could be found in that fossil?

LOOK!

It is found …

They are found …

What is palaeontology?   It is …

Wider world
City animals

22 **Read. Match the words in blue to the photos.**

1 Helen, UK

The animals that I see are not in the Natural History Museum! Londoners and visitors can often see lots of wild animals in the parks. At night, some people have seen **foxes** in the outskirts! Did you know that foxes play with their prey before they eat it?

2 Laxmi, India

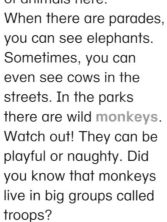

I live in New Delhi, the capital of India. You can see lots of animals here. When there are parades, you can see elephants. Sometimes, you can even see cows in the streets. In the parks there are wild **monkeys**. Watch out! They can be playful or naughty. Did you know that monkeys live in big groups called troops?

3 Carlos, Argentina

Here in Buenos Aires a lot of people have dogs as pets. There are many dog walkers, that is, people who walk the dogs while their owners are working. There is a large Nature Reserve close to the city where you can see frogs and **weasels**. Did you know that weasels change the colour of their fur coat according to the season?

a

b

c

23 **Ask and answer.**

What wild animals can you see in these big cities?

1 Do you think wild animals can be a problem in a big city? Why?

2 What animal do you think is the most interesting?

3 Why do you think weasels change the colour of their fur?

4 What interesting wild animals can you see where you live?

PORTFOLIO

Think and write.

Find out about a strange and interesting animal.
Then write about it.

24 **Read and say.**

Hello, I'm Hannah. I'm studying to be a vet. I don't like working in offices, but I love working with animals. I like camping, too. I'm good at climbing and pitching tents. I'm working as a youth leader at an adventure camp. Last summer I went to Brazil. I was a youth leader at Camp Paulo. It was very hot in Brazil, but there were a lot of interesting animals.

1	Hannah is studying to be a …	**a** cook	**b** vet	**c** youth leader
2	She's good at ….	**a** climbing	**b** trampolining	**c** diving
3	Last summer Hannah went to …	**a** Argentina	**b** England	**c** Brazil
4	It was very … at Camp Paulo.	**a** cold	**b** hot	**c** rainy
5	There were lots of interesting … there.	**a** insects	**b** flowers	**c** animals

25 **Look at the pictures. Then ask and answer.**

Picture A

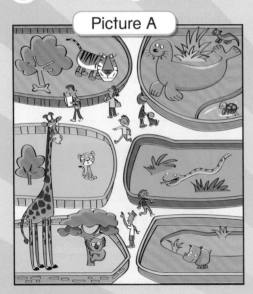

Picture B

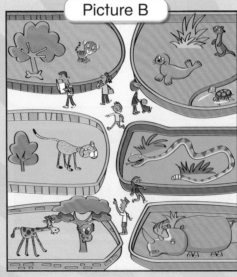

1 Which picture has the longest snake?
2 In which picture is the giraffe taller than the rhino?
3 Which picture has the biggest tiger?
4 In which picture is the turtle the smallest?

26 **Play the memory game.**

I went to the wildlife park and I saw a rhino.

I went to the wildlife park and I saw a rhino and a crocodile.

Picture Dictionary

AB p.105

27 **Listen and point.**

1

longer shorter

2

bigger faster

3

lighter taller

4

fastest faster

5

fastest heaviest

6

lightest biggest

28 **Read and say.**

1 One of the snakes is the *(more / most / fast)* dangerous in the world.

2 The giraffe is five *(metres / kilogrammes / heavy)* tall.

3 It can't run, *(does / but / and)* it can climb trees.

4 *(Where / Which / How)* animal is the lightest?

29 **Read and ask.**

Animals

Ask B:

1 Are giraffes taller than camels?

2 Are seals heavier than whales?

3 Are cheetahs faster than gorillas?

4 Lemurs, otters or cats: which animal is the smallest?

Ask A:

1 Are whales longer than seals?

2 Are elephants heavier than whales?

3 Are snakes slower than turtles?

4 Rhinos, cheetahs or lemurs: which animal is the heaviest?

3 Where we live

1 🎵 1:40 **Listen and read. What's Flo doing?**

Phew! 450 steps!

I'm hot now! I want to go swimming! Where's the swimming pool?

It's there – behind the cinema. But where's Flo?

Oh no! She's got the money!

Look! She's there – near the park. What's she doing?

She's buying an ice cream. I want an ice cream, too! Come on!

2 🎵 1:41 **Listen and repeat.**

1 shopping centre

2 post office

3 cinema

4 chemist

5 newsagent

6 college

7 circus

8 factory

9 theatre

3 (1:42) **Listen and point.**

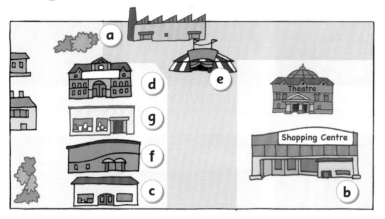

LOOK!

How do you get to the swimming pool?

Turn left at the corner, then go straight ahead.

The swimming pool is inside the sports centre, at the end of the building.

1 post office **5** college

2 cinema **6** circus

3 chemist **7** factory

4 newsagent

4 (1:43) **Listen and choose the right picture.**

1

2

3

5 **Ask and answer.**

near   between   next to   behind   straight ahead   at the end of   in front of

1 How do you get from the college to the cinema?

2 How do you get from the shopping centre to the circus?

3 Where should you go to post a letter / buy a newspaper / watch a film?

6 🔊 1:45 **Listen and repeat.**

1
university

2
airport

3
bookshop

4
fire station

5
police station

6
railway station

7
bus stop

8
guest house

9
stadium

10
underground

7 🔊 1:46 **Listen to the song. Clap when you hear the words in blue.**

SONG

Girl: I want to go to the shopping centre.
Do you want to come with me?
Boy: Sorry, I can't, my friend.
I want to go to the shopping centre,
But I have to do other things.

[Chorus]

Boy: *There are many things I want to do.*
But I can't, my friend. I can't today.
I have to go to the bookshop.
I have to go to the post office.
I have to go to the airport, *to pick*
up a friend.

Girl: I want to go to the theatre.
Do you want to come with me?
Boy: Sorry, I can't, my friend.
I want to go to the theatre,
But I have to do other things.

[Chorus]

Girl: I want to go to the circus.
Do you want to come with me?
Boy: Sorry, I can't, my friend.
I want to go to the circus,
But I have to do other things.

8 **Read the song and say.**

1 Where does the girl want to go?

2 Where does the boy have to go?

LOOK!

I want to go to the park.
He/She wants to go to the library.
She has to go to the shopping centre. She needs to get the underground.
If you walk to the park, you will find the shop at the end of the street.
If she needs to go to the library, she should/needs to go by bus.

9 **Read and say.**

	Who?	Wants to go …	Will have to …
1	Michael	bookshop	catch the bus
2	Katy	airport	get a train
3	Anna	stadium	walk
4	William	guest house	get a taxi
5	Maya	university	ride a bicycle
6	Robert	factory	drive a car

> If Michael wants to go to the bookshop, he will have to catch the bus.

10 **Ask and answer.**

1 How do you get there?

2 If a friend of yours wants to go there, how can he/she get there?

3 Where will he/she find the place?

> Where do you need to go every day?

11 Look at the pictures. Tell the story.

12 🔊 1:48 Listen and find out. Are there animals on Future Island? Then act out.

1

This is my house.

I'm **hungry**!

Do you like fish and chips?

2

Here you are!

Oh, er ... thanks! Is this your dog?

FISH

CHIPS

3

Yes. He's a robot. There **aren't** any real pets.

4

What? There **aren't** any **animals** here?

All the animals are dead.

5

zero ZENDELL'S ZOO

Zero Zendell's got some animals.

THAT'S HIM!! THE MAN WITH THE TIME MACHINE! HE'S GOT CHAMP!!

6

What?! Champ is in Zero Zendell's **zoo**?!

7

Let's go and **rescue** him!

VALUES

Learn to be flexible! It's often frustrating to have to do what you don't want to do.

HOME-SCHOOL LINK

Tell your family how to be flexible.

PARENT

Suffixes –ful and –ly

Suffixes are groups of letters that we add to the end of a word to change it.

To form adjectives from nouns:

• peace → peaceful, friend → friendly

To form adverbs from adjectives:

• quick → quickly, slow → slowly

Be careful! There are some irregular spellings:

• happy → happily, beauty → beautiful

---

13 **Listen and repeat.**

-ful -ly

14 **Listen, point and say.**

1	2	3
noun + ful	noun + ly	adjective + ly

friend → friendly   care → careful   quick → quickly
strange → strangely careful → carefully kind → kindly
easy → easily   colour → colourful   soft → softly

---

15 **Listen and read. Then repeat.**

1 The city is very colourful.
2 She drove very dangerously in the neighbourhood.
3 They welcomed me so warmly into their home.
4 She is very thankful for the theatre tickets.
5 I learnt the recipe very easily.
6 I'm so forgetful! I need to go to the bookshop.

16 **Read and blend the words with a partner.**

-ful	-ly
beauty → beautiful	easy → easily
care → careful	happy → happily
play → playful	life → lively

---

17 **Listen and repeat.**

It was a beautiful day.
When suddenly I heard 'Be careful!'
But it was too late.

18 **Read and answer.**

left   right   urban   rural   population   east   west   north   south

1 What are the differences between towns or cities and villages?
2 Are there more inhabitants in cities or in villages nowadays?
3 Why do you sometimes need a map?
4 What do maps often have in the corner?

The number of inhabitants in a place is called the population. One of the biggest differences between a town or city and a village is the population. People who live in a town or city are called the urban population and those living in a village are called the rural population. If you look at the graph below you will see that in 1900 the rural population used to be larger than the urban population. However, in 2000, the urban population was larger than the rural population.

Towns and cities can be very big and so it's helpful to have a map. Most maps have a compass in the corner which tells you if you are in the north, south, east or west of the city. Maps also help you to know if you should turn left or right. If you visit a big city like London and want to visit the tourist sites, having a map will stop you getting lost!

19 **Look and find the right description for the graph.**

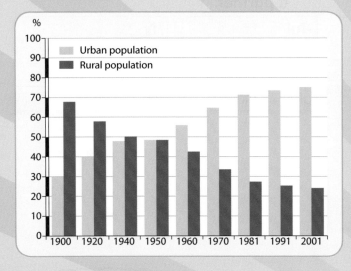

1 In 1900 the rural population was more than 50% and the urban population was under 20%.
In 2001 the rural population continued being more than 50% but the urban population had increased notably up to 70%.

2 In 1900 the rural population was over 60% and the urban population was under 40%.
In 2001 the rural population was under 30% but the urban population had increased notably up to 75%.

3 In 1900 the rural population was over 30% and the urban population was 60%.
In 2001 the rural population continued being no more than 30% but the urban population had increased notably up to 75%.

20 **Do you live in a town, city or village? Tell your partner.**

1 What did your town, city or village use to be like?
2 Where do you prefer to live? Why?
3 What will you see if you go to a big city like London?

It used to be very busy.

Wider world
Our homes

21 **Read. Match the texts to the photos.**

1

I live on an island in Greece called Paros. I live with my family in a beautiful white house in a village. The island is quite small – just 13,000 people live here. There is a harbour near our house. We like sailing and sometimes we go fishing with our father. My father loves fishing but he's not very good at it! I love living on an island.

Eleni, 12, Greece

a

2

I'm from a small town in Andalucía, Spain. My house is very unusual. It's a cave house. Some people think caves are scary and dark but I think they're great. A lot of people go to the beautiful beaches at the weekend. It's fun to play volleyball on the sand. The old castles near my house are very interesting, too. My favourite is called Vélez-Blanco. I love my home!

Alba, 11, Spain

b

3

I live in Hong Kong, a very busy place in Asia. Seven million people live in Hong Kong. I live on the fortieth floor of a building in Kowloon. It's got great views. There's a sports centre behind my flat. There are a lot of shopping centres, restaurants and museums near my home. The Science Museum is my favourite. I always learn new and interesting things there. I love Hong Kong!

Chiu-Wai, 12, China

c

22 🔊 1:54 **Listen and read. Then answer the questions.**

1 Where does Alba live? What about Chiu-Wai and Eleni?

2 How are Andalucía, Hong Kong and Paros different?

3 Why do you think that many houses are white in Spain and Greece?

PORTFOLIO

Think and write.

Where did you use to live when you were little? Write a mini autobiography with your first memories of home.

23 **Look at the map. Read and say** *True* **or** *False*.

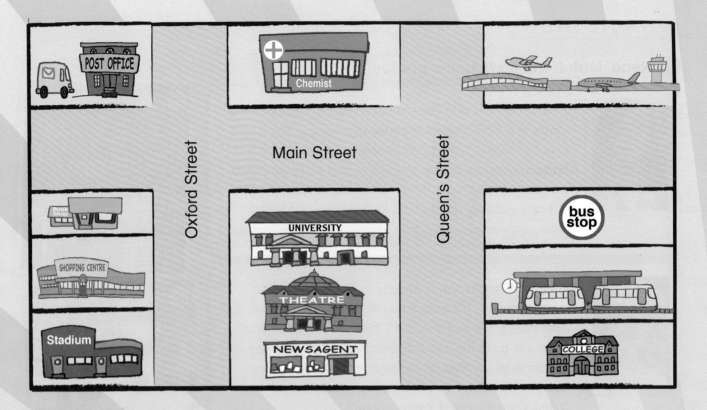

1 The stadium is opposite the newsagent.

2 The theatre is between the university and the newsagent.

3 The college is near the bookshop.

4 The bus stop is next to the railway station.

5 If you go from the stadium to the airport, you need to go straight ahead on Oxford Street. Then you need to turn to right. The airport is at the end of Main Street.

6 Make up two sentences that are true.

7 Make up two sentences that are false.

24 **Read and choose the right word.**

1 If you have to go the airport, you *(should / want)* leave at 5 o'clock.

2 If you *(will / visit)* the library, you'll find new book titles.

3 If they *(went / go)* to the shopping centre, they'll buy some ice cream.

4 You *(will / can)* like the stadium if you visit it.

AB p.106

25 **Ask and answer.**

1 What can you see both in a city and a village?
2 What can you see only in the city?
3 Where do you live, in a city, town or village?
4 How do you get from school to your home?

26 **Play the guessing game.**

It's a place where you can see films.

Is it a cinema?

It's a place where you can buy books.

Is it a bookshop?

27 **Read and ask.**

A

B

Ask B:

1 Can you buy medicines at the chemist?
2 Can you watch a play at the cinema?
3 Can you buy sweets at the newsagent?
4 Where you can learn something new?

Ask A:

1 Can you see a show at the circus?
2 Can you stay overnight in a guest house?
3 Can you post a letter at the chemist?
4 Where can you get transport to other places?

Good and bad days

1 🔊 2:01 **Listen and read. How does Tom feel?**

1 Tom, what's wrong?

I'm hungry!

2 I was asleep and missed lunch. I wanted an omelette but there weren't any eggs.

3 Then I wanted some spaghetti but the box was too high.

4 I cooked a curry but then I dropped the plate on the grass.

5 Don't worry, have some of my paella!

Yum! Thank you!

2 🔊 2:02 **Listen and repeat.**

1 curry
2 omelette
3 spaghetti
4 fish and chips
5 paella
6 dumplings
7 sushi
8 stew
9 rice and beans

3 **Ask and answer.**

What happened to his curry?

What happened to Tom first when he wanted an omelette?

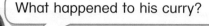

Did he like Felipe's paella?

LOOK!

I **cooked** a stew.	He **dropped** the plate.
	We **fell** in the lake.
She **paddled** very fast.	We **ate** an omelette.

4 (2:03) **Listen and look. Then say who is in the pictures and what they are doing.**

Hannah cooked omelettes.

5 **Read these sentences. *True* or *False*?**

1 Tom went to the big lake in the forest.
2 Hannah cooked some omelettes.
3 Tom paddled very slowly.
4 Maria was too scared to climb up the climbing wall.

6 **Look at Activity 5. Put the sentences in the right order. Use the words in the box.**

first   then   next   last

7 **Think about what you did yesterday / last week / a year ago / in 2010 / last month. Tell your partner.**

8 🔊 2:04 **Listen and repeat.**

① pack my bag **②** miss the bus **③** pass a test **④** open a lunchbox **⑤** remember my juice **⑥** drop the ball

9 🔊 2:05 **Listen to the song. Which words are missing?**

dropped the ball   remember my juice   pass my test   missed the bus

SONG

It was a bad day, it was really bad
But you smiled at me, now I'm not sad.

I packed my school bag and walked up the street.
I (1) ... , 'Ow, my tired feet.'
I didn't (2) ... , I was late for class.
My friends said, 'Next time, get here fast!'
I opened my lunchbox and said, 'No way!'
I didn't (3) ... today.

Chorus

I went to the park and played with a ball.
I kicked it too hard, it went over a wall.
A boy helped me, he didn't ask why.
We played in the park and we looked at the sky.
I (4) ... , he said, 'That's OK.'
Now he's my friend and it's a good day.

10 Read and say. *True* or *False*?

1 She didn't miss the bus.
2 She was late for class.
3 She remembered her juice.
4 She didn't kick a ball.
5 She dropped the ball.

11 Read and say.

> We didn't laugh because we were sad.

1 We/*not laugh*/because we were sad.
2 She/*not open*/her eyes because it was a scary film.
3 They/*play*/a second football match because they weren't tired.
4 I/*pass*/the test because I revised a lot.
5 He/*not miss*/the bus because he was early.

LOOK!

| What happened? | I **didn't** pass my test because I **didn't** revise. **It made me sad!** |
| | I **played** tennis with my friends because it **didn't** rain. **It made me happy!** |

12 **Read and say the right word.**

1 I passed my English test. It made me *(proud / embarrassed)*.
2 She played football all day. It made her *(sad / tired)*.
3 His mum prepared a delicious plate of spaghetti. It made him *(happy / angry)*.
4 They couldn't play in the park because it was too cold. It made them *(nervous / sad)*.

13 (2:06) **Listen and answer.**

1 Emma   **2** Sally and John   **3** Sam and Sue   **4** Peter   **5** Jim and Simon

1 Why didn't Emma catch the ball?
2 Why didn't Sally and John pass the test?
3 Why didn't Sam and Sue swim in the sea?
4 Why didn't Peter eat the curry?
5 Why didn't Jim and Simon play football?

14 **Look at Activity 13 and answer.**

1 What happened when the sun was in Emma's eyes?
2 What happened when Sally and John didn't study a lot?
3 What happened when Sam and Sue saw the red flag in the sea?

15 **Ask and answer. What didn't you do? Why?**

I didn't play football because I was tired.

16 Look at the pictures. Tell the story.

17 (2:08) Listen and find out. Is Champ all right? Then act out.

VALUES

Be positive about your day.
Don't worry. Be happy!

HOME-SCHOOL LINK

Show good manners at the table.

Simple past of regular verbs '–ed' review.

It is pronounced:
• /t/ after unvoiced sounds.
• /d/ after voiced sounds.
• /id/ after verbs ending –t or –d.

18 **2:09 Listen and repeat.**

/t/ /d/ /id/

19 **2:10 Listen and point at the endings. Then say the odd one out.**

1 played, followed, visited.

2 decided, painted, packed.

3 ended, stopped, missed.

4 collected, lived, recorded.

5 passed, watched, opened.

6 revised, remembered, dropped.

20 Ask and answer.

1 Where did you play chess yesterday?
I played …

2 What did you listen to in the music lesson last week? I listened …

3 How did you revise for the test?
I revised …

4 Where did you study last night?
I studied …

5 What did you watch on TV on Sunday?
I watched …

6 When did you decide to go?
I decided …

7 Who did you visit last week?
I visited …

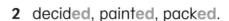
Where did you play chess yesterday?

21 **2:11 Listen and repeat.**

SOUNDS FUN!

Donny wanted the ball but he passed it on to Ted.
Ted played fast but it bounced off the teacher's head!

22 **Look at the picture. Then answer the questions.**

> nutrients   sedentary   physical activity
> vitamins   minerals

1 Are they friends or married? How do you know?
2 Do they look the same age? Why?
3 What does Sam look like? And Emma?

Name: Emma
Surname: Robins

Name: Sam
Surname: Robins

Healthy habits

Look at the couple in the picture. They have been married since 1990! The husband looks much older than the wife. Why? Read their stories and find out.

Emma
When we were younger my husband was always trying new dishes and was very interested in international food. However, this was just an excuse… I soon realised that he had a sedentary lifestyle because he was eating too much and wasn't doing enough exercise. I asked him to go to the gym with me but he was always too busy for physical activity.

Sam
We got married after only 6 months of engagement. I still remember the first dinner she cooked for us: a salad, full of vitamins and minerals. I was mixing the salad when she said 'I love … salads'! Oh yes she does! She loves sports and any food full of nutrients.

23 **Read these sentences about healthy habits and choose a or b.**

1 **a** Health is important for all ages.
  b Health is only a problem for the elderly.

3 **a** Physical activity keeps your body healthy.
  b Physical activity is only for fun.

2 **a** If you are sedentary, you are very active.
  b If you are sedentary, you are inactive.

4 **a** Fruits and vegetables are full of fat.
  b Fruits and vegetables are full of vitamins and minerals.

24 **What were they doing right and wrong? Tell your partner.**

LOOK!

> She was eating vegetables.
> They were doing physical activity.

> Sam wasn't doing much physical activity.

Wider world
Food traditions

25 **Read and match the words in blue to the pictures.**

a

b

c

d

e

f

Naoko, Japan

Here in Japan we don't use knives and forks for ours meals. It is our custom to eat meals with **chopsticks**. We do use a type of spoon when we have soup and stew. Another tradition in Japan is the tea ceremony. Husbands, wives, grandparents and children come together for a formal gathering where green tea is served. Women wear traditional **kimonos**.

Charlotte, Sweden

We have many Swedish traditions in the different seasons. In August it is summer time in Sweden. This is the time when families get together for a **crayfish** party. We decorate our gardens with **paper lanterns**. We wear funny crayfish hats and bibs so that we don't get dirty. I like eating the crayfish with my hands!

Geoffrey, USA

In the USA we have many food traditions. One of them is the **barbecue**. This is something that we do when we have parties and celebrations and the weather is nice. We cook sausages and steak on the barbecue, then everyone enjoys the meal. Another American tradition associated with a fire is roasting chestnuts. People roast **chestnuts** on an open fire when the weather is cold. This is a fun thing in autumn too, but I prefer roasting them in winter!

26 **Ask and answer.**

> What do they use to eat in Japan? What do you use?

> Why do you think people have celebrations outdoors in Sweden and the USA?

27 **Which of these traditions do you like the best? Why?**

> Do you have a similar tradition in your country?

PORTFOLIO

Think and write.

Write a report about food traditions in your country.

28 **Play the game.**

 **HAVE FUN!**

	yesterday	last week	last month	last year	an hour ago	two days ago	

FINISH | **28** missed | **27** Did you brush your teeth? | **26** | **25** played

20 | **21** climbed | **22** Did you wash the dishes? | **23** got | **24** Did you do your homework?

19 made | **18** ate | **17** | **16** | **15** Did you get up late?

10 Did you miss the bus? | **11** | **12** Did you help your friend? | **13** Did you make your bed yesterday? | **14** brought

9 drank | **8** | **7** | **6** went | **5**

START | **1** wrote | **2** saw | **3** Did you take out the rubbish? | **4** dropped

Picture Dictionary

AB p.107

29   **2:14 Listen and answer.**

What happened?		
1 Mandy		
2 Greg		
3 Eric		
4 Joan		

a Why was Mandy late for school? Why do you think she failed the Maths test?

b Why was Greg hungry at lunchtime?

c Where did Eric kick the ball over the wall?

d What made Joan unhappy?

30 Read and ask.

A

Read to B:

I like cooking. I went to a cookery school last year. I cooked many kinds of dishes at the school. After making the dishes we wrote how to make them in our notebooks. I made a Spanish dish called paella. It had rice and seafood in it. I also made an omelette. It's made from eggs.

Ask B:

1 Do I like cooking?

2 What did I do last year?

3 What dishes did I prepare?

4 What did I use to make paella?

B

Read to A:

I don't like cooking that much. I like going to restaurants. My favourite dishes are hot and spicy. Last week I went to a restaurant and I ordered curry. It's a very popular food in India and some Asian On my birthday, I ate a really hot curry and drank about two litres of water!

Ask A:

1 Do I like cooking?

2 What did I do last week?

3 What kind of food did I have?

4 Why did I drink so much water on my birthday?

1 🔘 2:15 **Listen and read. Why does Flo say sorry to Maria?**

1 Hi, Maria!

Hi guys! I just saw **Shadow in the House**. It's a scary thriller but I had a great time!

2 There was something in the house. It wrote letters on the window ...

3 ... and it made terrible noises.

4 Boo! Aaah! Flo, we didn't see you!

5 Sorry!

2 🔘 2:16 **Listen and repeat.**

1 thriller
2 comedy
3 sci-fi
4 romance
5 musical
6 cartoon

3 **Ask and answer.**

What kind of films do you prefer?

Which kind of films would you rather not see?

4 **Read and answer. Use the words in the box.**

Yes, it did   Yes, she did   No, she didn't
Yes, she did   No, it didn't

I watched the film **by myself.**

You wrote it **by yourself, didn't you**?

He made it **by himself, didn't he**?

She didn't go to the cinema **by herself, did she**?

They didn't draw it **by themselves, did they**?

1 Maria watched a scary film, didn't she?
2 Maria had a good time, didn't she?
3 The shadow didn't write on the window, did it?
4 The shadow made friendly noises, didn't it?
5 Flo didn't watch the film, did she?

5 **Listen and answer the questions. Use the words in the box.**

No, he didn't   Yes, they did   No, she didn't   Yes, he did

1 The boy wrote the letter by himself, didn't he?

2 The girl played by herself, didn't she?

3 They made dinner by themselves, didn't they?

4 He didn't watch the film by himself, did he?

6 **Read and ask your partner.**

1 you / write / in your diary / last week

2 you / watch / film / last Saturday

3 you / make / dinner for your family / yesterday

4 you / not forget / your homework / this morning

5 you/ not have / a birthday party / last year

You wrote in your diary last week, didn't you?

7  **Listen and repeat.**

1 cello

2 harmonica

3 saxophone

4 triangle

5 drums

6 clarinet

7 harp

8 tambourine

8 **Listen and guess. What instrument is it?**

9 **Listen and repeat.**
Do you know any other kinds of music?

SONG

10 **Listen to the song. How many instruments are there in the song?**

Chorus:
Did you hear the music last night on the radio?
I didn't feel happy, I was so sad.
But the music was great, it made me feel glad.

Chorus:
Did you hear the music last night on the radio?
Yes, I did. Playing funky jazz was a saxophone.
And I loved dancing to it on my own.

Chorus:
Did you hear the music last night on the radio?
No, I didn't. Was it pop, was it rock, what was it like?
Country music with guitars and violins, it was all right.

Chorus:
Did you hear the music last night on the radio?
Yes, I did. It was the kind of music I choose.
Guitar and harmonica playing the blues.

11 **Ask and answer.**

What kind of music
do you dislike?

What kind of
music do you like?

Can you play an
instrument?

TIP!
on my own = by myself

LOOK!

Have you ever played the saxophone?	Yes, **I've played** it **since** I was 7.
Have you heard that song **yet**?	Yes, **I've just heard** it on the radio.
How long have you been at the concert?	**I've been** here **for** 2 hours.

12 2:24 Look, listen and match.

a

b

c

d

1 He's been at the restaurant for 10 minutes.

2 He got 100%.

3 She's played chess with her grandad since she was 7.

4 He's just arrived from Australia.

5 He hasn't been to the cinema for a long time.

e

TIP!

already = before now
I have already done my homework

13 Read and answer.

1 Have you ever got 100% in a test?

2 Have you ever been to a different country?

3 How long have you been at school?

4 Have you seen a good film recently?

14 Unscramble. Then say.

1 you / been / London / have / to?

2 finished / just / have / we / books / our.

3 been / UK / in / the / I / have / 4 / years / for.

4 visited / have / Turkey / you?

15 Look at the pictures. Tell the story.

16 (2:26) Listen and find out. Where will the underground river take Marta, Chris and Serena? Then act out.

1
What can we do? How can we rescue Champ?

It's difficult...

ZOO

2
Wait! I know this place! Isn't it the nature reserve?

What? Here?

3
THE LAST NATURE RESERVE ON THE ISLAND WAS HERE IT CLOSED 100 YEARS AGO

4
My parents started this nature reserve. There was an underground river!

Where?

5
Here! It was easy to bring food for the animals ... we used the river!

Where did it go?

It went from the harbour, past the zoo, and into the nature reserve!

NATURE RESERVE
ZOO
HARBOUR

6
Yes! And we can use it! We can get into Zero Zendell's Zoo!

Cool! It's the river!

VALUES

Learn to be self-sufficient! You can always do some things by yourself.

HOME-SCHOOL LINK

Tell your family about the things that you can do by yourself. PARENT

Adding prefixes

Prefixes are groups of letters we add to the beginning of a word which change the meaning:

- un/dis/im/il/ir mean 'not' → untidy, disagree, impolite, illegal, irresponsible
- pre means 'before' → precook, preheat, preview
- re means 'again' → reuse, rewrite, reread

17 **Listen and repeat.**

1 **un-** → untidy, unhealthy
2 **dis-** → dislike, disorder
3 **im-** → impossible, impersonal
4 **re-** → react, reread
5 **pre-** → prehistoric, prepay
6 **i-** → illegal, irregular
7 **in-** → informal, indiscreet

18 **Listen, point and say.**

unhappy – happy
appear – disappear
visible – invisible
recycle – cycle
cook – precook
irresponsible – responsible

19 **Read and blend the words with a partner.**

un-	dis-	im-	re-	pre-	i-	in-
tidy	like	possible	cycle	historic	llegal	visible
happy	appear	personal	act	pay	rregular	discreet
healthy	order	polite	call	cook	rresponsible	formal
fit	agree	mature	write	heat	rresistible	credible

20 **Listen and repeat.**

It is irresponsible, impolite
and unkind
to leave the actor behind!

21 (2:31) **Listen and match.**

rock

blues

country

pop

jazz

a Can you hear the dialogue between the voice and the **guitar**? This is the Blues. The Blues was born in the USA. Blues was influenced by African music and it has been the basis for many other popular music genres including jazz, country and rock!

b Listen to the **trumpet** and try to follow the rhythm. It isn't easy because each Jazz performer plays the tune in their own way!

c The guitar, **drum** and bass, did you hear them? Since 1950, rock singers have sung their songs accompanied by these instruments. There are many different types of rock that are very popular nowadays.

d Folk and gospel are the roots of country music. This music was very popular among young people in the 1970s in the USA. Country singers usually write their own songs and have beautiful **voices**.

e Pop music originated in Britain in the late 1950's and can be described as commercial music for a young audience. Its easy listening makes it very accessible to everyone. That's why it's called popular music!

22 **Ask and answer.**

1 How do people listen to music nowadays?
2 What type of music do you usually listen to? And your parents and friends?
3 What other types of music do you know?

23 **Read Activity 21 again and complete. Choose one word from the box.**

blues   country   jazz   pop   rock

1 I was listening to … music, when I heard a drum solo.
2 They were listening to … music, when they heard a beautiful voice.
3 I was listening to … music, when I saw people dancing.
4 They were listening to … music, when they heard a trumpet solo.
5 I was listening to … music, when I heard an African rhythm.

How did people listen to music 20 years ago?

They used tape recorders.

LOOK!

I was listening to the radio when she arrived.

They were playing the guitar when I called.

Wider world
World instruments

24 **Read and match the paragraphs to the photos.**

1

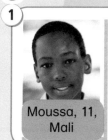

Moussa, 11, Mali

I live in Mali, Africa. **Djembe** drums are very famous in my country. People made djembe drums more than 1,500 years ago. These drums are made of hard wood and goat's skin. Sometimes there are lovely pictures of animals or people on them, too. We like listening to the djembe drums and dancing. Today, people in Africa play these drums for special celebrations. Famous musicians around the world like playing the djembe drums, too.

2

Marta, 11, Argentina

I live in Buenos Aires, Argentina. People in my country play an instrument called the bandoneon. A **bandoneon** player pushes and pulls on the instrument to make beautiful music. It has square boxes at each end. The boxes are made of wood and have seventy-one buttons on them. Each button can play two different notes. The bandoneon is very difficult to play. It can take ten years to learn. We play the bandoneon when people dance the tango. It's great music for dancing!

3

Takahiro, 12, Japan

I'm from Okinawa in Japan. A famous insrument in my country is the **shamisen**. It's like a guitar with a long thin neck but the body is like a tambourine covered in snake's skin or paper and it only has three strings. People play it with a short piece of wood.

Sometimes people sing when they play the shamisen. Street singers use the shamisen to tell stories. People use it in theatre, too. Today, some Japanese rock bands also play this instrument.

25 **Ask and answer.**

> When do people play the bandoneon, shamisen and djembe?

> They play these instruments at special celebrations.

1 How are these instruments similar and different?

3 What other materials can instruments be made of?

2 What are they made of?

4 Which instruments do you think are the most difficult to play?

PORTFOLIO

Think and write.

Make a list of some instruments and where they are from.
Write a report about other instruments from around the world.

26 **Think about traditional instruments in your country. When do people play them? Then talk with your partner.**

HAVE FUN!

FINISH

17 Have you ever played the harp?

16 Have you ever played in a band?

15 They were watching television when _____.

18 Have you ever been to a concert?

12 Have you ever eaten popcorn at the cinema?

14 Have you ever made a birthday cake?

11 They didn't draw it by themselves, _____?

13 He watched a scary film, _____?

9 Have you ever seen a musical at the theatre?

8 Have you ever been late for school?

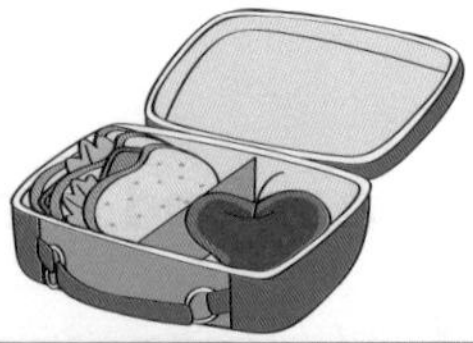

7 Have you ever watched a sci-fi film?

10 What was the weather like yesterday?

6 Did you eat all your lunch yesterday?

1 Did you come to school today by yourself?

3 Did you help your friends today?

2 Have you ever listened to an English song?

START

5 I _____ when I saw my friend Sarah.

4 Which do you prefer: a comedy, a thriller, or a cartoon?

Picture Dictionary

AB p.108

28 (2:33) **Listen and point to two items.**

Have you ever …?

1 Ann	a		b		c	
2 Dave	a		b		c	

29 **Read and say the question tag.**

1 You went to piano lessons last year, …?
2 She didn't like the romantic film, …?
3 He played the drums at the concert, …?
4 They didn't like the jazz festival, …?

30 **Read and ask.**

A

Read to B:

I've played the harp since I was 7. I've played it for 5 years. I always liked how it sounded. It has taken me 4 years to learn how to play songs. At first, it was difficult, but I've become very good at it. I haven't forgotten the first song that I learned.

Ask B:

1 How long have I played the harp?
2 I always liked it, didn't I?
3 How long has it taken me to learn how to play songs?
4 At first it was difficult, wasn't it?

B

Read to A:

I've watched many kinds of films, but I've never seen a thriller. Last year I watched a scary film by myself and I didn't enjoy it. I was too scared! I've haven't been to the cinema yet. They've just opened a new one near my house and I can't wait to go.

Ask A:

1 What kind of film haven't I seen?
2 I watched a scary film last year, didn't I? Did I enjoy it?
3 Have I ever been to the cinema?
4 Where is the new cinema?

6 Trips

1 (2:34) **Listen and read. Where was Felipe yesterday?**

1
Hi, there! There was an old ticket for Aquafun water park in the tent. Is it yours?

No, it isn't ours. We went to the palace yesterday.

2
Maria, did you go to Aquafun yesterday?

No, I didn't. I went to the museum.

3
Felipe, did you go to Aquafun yesterday?

Really?!

Yes, I did. It was amazing!

2 (2:35) **Listen and repeat.**

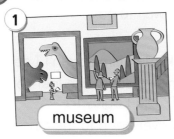

1 museum

2 aquarium

3 amusement park

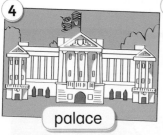

4 palace

5 water park

6 castle

7 National Park

3 **Read and sort. Put the places in order from your most to your least favourite.**

LOOK!

What **will** you do tomorrow?	First, **I'll** go to the castle.
	Then, **I'll** go to the museum.
	Last, **I'll** go to the water park!

4 🔊 2:36 **Look and listen. Then answer.**

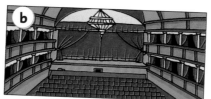

1 Where will he go first, next and last?   **2** Where will she go first, next and last?

3 Where will she go first, next and last?

5 **Ask and answer.**

> Will Maria go to the museum? Yes, she will!

1  **?**   **2**  **?**

3  **?**   **4**  **?**

6 **Think about what you will do. Then talk to your partner.**

Where will you go after school? What will you do?

Where will you go next weekend? What will you do?

7  **Listen and repeat.**

1 
go on the
big wheel

2 
go on the
dodgems

3 
play
mini-golf

4 
go on the
carousel

5 
go on the
boating lake

6 
go on the
rollercoaster

7 
go on the
pirate ship

8 
go on the
water slide

8 **2:38** **Listen to the song. What rides did they like?**

SONG

We went to the theme park yesterday,
A special treat for my brother's birthday.
Did you like the big wheel, going up high?
No, I didn't! Because I can't fly!

Did you like the carousel, with horses of gold?
No, the horses were small and we're too old!
Did you like the dodgems then, fun and fast?
No, we didn't! Our car was slow and we were last.

So where did you go? What rides did you like?
Did you like the mini-golf and the boating lake?
No, but we loved the rollercoaster, it was a thrill.
We went on it ten times and now we feel ill!

9 **Read and say in the future.**

We went to the amusement
park yesterday.

We'll go to the amusement
park tomorrow.

1 We loved the rollercoaster →
2 The dodgems were fast →
3 Mini-golf is great →
4 The carousel is slow →

TIP!

theme park = amusement park

Shall we go on the big wheel? I'm not sure.

What else **could** we do? We **could** go on the rollercoaster.

 10 2:39 **Look and listen. Then point and answer. Where are they going next?**

1 a  b  c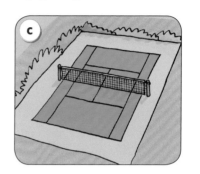

2 a  b 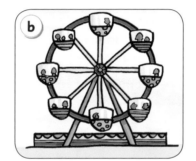 c

3 a  b  c

11 **Unscramble and say.**

1 visit / museum / on / the / shall / we / Friday?

2 could / what / else / do / we?

3 sure / I / not / am.

4 dodgems / we / on / shall / go / the ?

12 **Make your own plans. Then talk to your partner.**

Shall we play mini-golf?

What else could we do?

13 Look at the pictures. Tell the story.

14 Listen and read. Why do people on Future Island admire Zero Zendell? Then act out.

VALUES

 Plan, but be flexible! Planning helps you do more things.

HOME-SCHOOL LINK

Help a family member plan their day.

Question tags and intonation

We can use question tags with different intonation.
- Rising intonation ↗ to ask for opinion.
- Falling intonation ↘ to ask for agreement.

Look at the difference:

It's cold, isn't it?   Yes, it is.

agreement ↗

It's cold, isn't it?   Not really!

opinion ↘

15 (2:43) **Listen and repeat.**

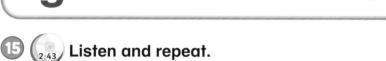

It's cold, isn't it? ↘

It's cold, isn't it? ↗

16 (2:44) **Listen and repeat. Then point.**

1 Your sister enjoyed the party, didn't she?

2 They can come together, can't they?

3 You are joking, aren't you?

4 It was very hot yesterday, wasn't it?

5 Peter wants to come with us, doesn't he?

18 (2:45) **Listen and repeat.**

17 **Ask and answer.**

You are Spanish, aren't you?   Yes, I am.

SOUNDS FUN!

It's sunny and hot today, isn't it?
Like in the pyramids in Egypt!

19 Read and find the words below in the text.

snow

rain

drought

fog

storm

Changes of weather

You are planning your holidays, booking a hotel, packing your suitcase when … oh no! It might rain! How do you know where to go and what to wear? Check the weather report! The air temperature tells you how hot or cold the weather is. Also, clouds can help tell you what the weather may be like at your destination.

Snow, rain, fog and storms all cause wet weather. If there is no rain for a long time then a drought may occur. Changes to the weather are measured with a rain gauge and thermometer. Put them outside in a safe place and record the results every day to make your own weather report!

Weather chart A

Day of the week	Rain	Temperature
Monday	Dry	25°
Tuesday	Dry	23°
Wednesday	Dry	23°
Thursday	Rainy	20°
Friday	Dry	26°

Weather chart B

Day of the week	Rain	Temperature
Monday	Rainy	3°
Tuesday	Snowy	0°
Wednesday	Snowy	0°
Thursday	Snowy	1°
Friday	Rainy	2°

20 Look at these weather charts. Is the weather wet or dry? What might you do in these places? Why?

1 In chart A …

2 In chart B …

21 Ask your partner. Use *may*.

1 I / open / window

2 he / go / with you

3 we / help / you

4 she / borrow / pencil

5 I / use / camera

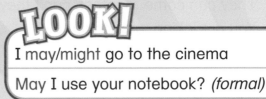

LOOK!

I may/might go to the cinema

May I use your notebook? *(formal)*

May I use your pen?

Wider world
Our holidays

22 **Read. Match the texts with the photos.**

a

1

Samir, 11, India

Last year, my family drove to a city called Agra in India. We visited the Taj Mahal. In our guidebook we read that Emperor Shah Jahan married a princess called Mumtaz Mahal. When she died, he was very sad. He built the Taj Mahal for her. Twenty-thousand workers used one thousand elephants and finished it in 1653. The tombs of Emperor Shah Jahan and his wife are inside the Taj Mahal. I need to buy an envelope and a stamp to send a letter and pictures to my grandma. She will think that the Taj Mahal is just incredible!

b

2

Zara, 12, Turkey

This summer, I went by bus to an ancient city in Turkey called Cappadocia. We stayed in a hotel in front of the Uçhisar Castle. During the day, I wrote a diary with all the details about our journey. In Cappadocia there are houses, restaurants, and hotels all inside the mountain. We then went in a hot-air balloon and saw the beautiful Fairy Chimneys. After that, we visited a famous Turkish bath. I'm looking forward to visiting Cappadocia again next year.

c

3

Juan, 12, Peru

Last year, I visited Cuzco. On our flight to Cuzco most of the passengers were tourists who wanted to see an amazing place called Machu Picchu. Cuzco is a busy place with lots of traffic, but then we took a taxi to a small mountain village called Aguas Calientes. Long ago, people called Incas had a city up in the Andean mountains. The city was lost there for hundreds of years until 1911 when an American professor discovered it. There are ruins of gardens, houses, and even a palace. We climbed up a mountain called Wayna Picchu where the guards of the city used to live. Machu Picchu is a great place to visit!

23 **Ask and answer.**

1 How did Samir, Zara and Juan get to their holiday places?
2 What is unusual about Capadoccia?
3 Who lived in Machu Picchu?
4 Why do you think the Incas built a city up in the mountains?

24 **Think about which of these three places you would like to visit. Tell your partner.**

PORTFOLIO

Think and say.

What is a nice place to visit where you live?
What activities can you do?
What's the weather like at different times of the year?

25 **Play the game.**

HAVE FUN!

Shall we visit the castle tomorrow?

He'll go on the big wheel.

key
→ = future with will
? = question

16 →
Make up your own sentence.

17 ?
Make up your own sentence.

18
Go back to 6

FINISH

15 ?
look for the palace

14 →
go / hiking / England / next / summer / we

13 ? visit the museum

12 →go/rollercoaster/ they/on/next/the

9 → go / I / Queen / the / to / palace / the / look for / to

8
Go back to 2

10 ?
Go shopping

11
Go up to 15

6 ? go on the dodgems

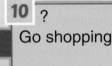

5 →
fly/London/he/ Wednesday/on

4 ?
play mini-golf at the weekend

7 ?
go to the cinema

START

1 ? go on the big wheel

2 →
read/ guidebook /next time/ she

3 →
aquarium/we/visit/ Monday/next

26 **Read and answer.**

1 You're lost in a different country. You look for a map, but you can't find one. What can you do?

2 You send a letter to your family. You don't know the name of the street and you can't remember the number. What can you do?

Picture Dictionary

AB p.109

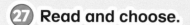

27 **Read and choose.**

1 *(Shall / Do / What)* we buy a guidebook for our trip?
2 What *(else / also / too)* could she see here?
3 She *(will / going / went)* go on the big wheel next.

28 **Unscramble and say.**

1 I / pencil / may / your / borrow ?
2 snows / might / skiing / we / if / go / it
3 open / may / I / window / the
4 cinema / I / go / tomorrow / to / might / the

29 **Read and ask.**

A

Read to B:

I think I'll fly to London next summer. First, I'll visit the museums and the palace. I love parks, so I'll spend some time there next. Perhaps we could go to see a play at the theatre – I love musicals!

Ask B:

1 Where do I think I will go next summer?
2 How will I get there?
3 What will I do first?
4 What will I do next?
5 What else do I want to do?

B

Read to A:

I think my mum and I will drive to Manchester next week. First, I'll visit a theme park that I like. Next, we'll spend the day in a water park because I love swimming. We could go to the cinema if we have time. I'm not sure.

Ask A:

1 Where do I think I will go next week?
2 How will I get there?
3 What will I do first?
4 What will I do next? Why do I want to go there?
5 What else do I want to do?

1 🔘 3:01 **Listen and read. What can they see?**

1 Felipe, why are you looking at the sky?

Because it's interesting. Look at the stars – they're beautiful.

2 Wow! What's that big red light?

Maybe it's a new star. Where is it?

3 Here. Maybe it's aliens!

4 Let me see! It isn't aliens, it's just a campfire on the hill.

Who is it?

It's Tom and Flo. Come on, let's go!

2 🔘 3:02 **Listen and repeat.**

1 astronaut
2 planet
3 telescope
4 alien
5 spaceship
6 comet
7 satellite
8 rocket
9 boosters
10 space station

3 **Read the story again. Find and say the questions for these answers.**

1 Because it's interesting.

3 Here.

2 Maybe it's a new star.

4 It's Tom and Flo.

LOOK!

We **should** go outside tonight to see the stars.

We'**d better** get ready. We **need** to take the telescope.

It's cold. We **ought to** wear our jackets!

4 (3:04) **Look and listen. Then point.**

5 **Unscramble and say.**

1 should / we / look / night / at / sky / the?

2 you/ better/ had / study / be / to / an / engineer / you / if / want.

3 ought / to / of / take / planet / care / we / Earth.

6 **Read and say. What do they need to do?**

1 It's cold outside. They don't want to catch a cold. They need to …

2 She has a test on the solar system. She doesn't want to fail. She needs to …

3 He gets to school late every day. He wakes up 20 minutes before school. He needs to …

7 **Ask and answer.**

What should you be good at to become an astronaut?

Where do you need to study?

8 **Listen and repeat.**

1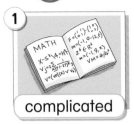
complicated

2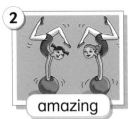
amazing

3
frightening

4
intelligent

5
brilliant

6
important

7
interesting

8
expensive

9
horrible

9  **Listen to the song. Does the astronaut like life in space?**

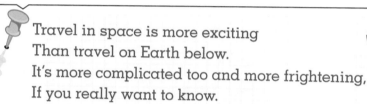

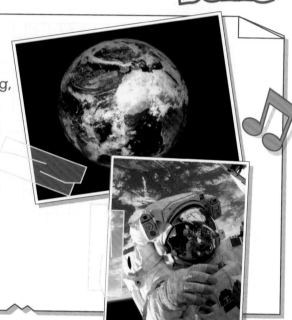

Travel in space is more exciting
Than travel on Earth below.
It's more complicated too and more frightening,
If you really want to know.

The question is – think about it,
Do aliens live out there?
And if they do, are they more intelligent
Than humans everywhere?

I don't know all the answers
But one thing I know is true,
That the world is an amazing place
And it's just right for me and you.

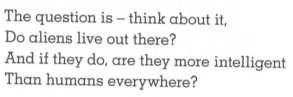

We say 'Oh dear!' when we are worried about something.
We say 'Really?' when we want to know more about something interesting or to express surprise.

10 **Read and say: 'Really?' or 'Oh dear!'**

1 I don't know all the answers.

2 I think that some aliens are more intelligent than humans.

3 I love learning about planets.

4 The planetarium was too expensive!

LOOK!

Which planet is more interesting?	The red planet is more interesting than the blue planet.
Which planet is the most interesting?	The red planet is the most interesting.
Which telescope is less complicated?	The small telescope is less complicated than the big telescope.
Which telescope is the least complicated?	The small telescope is the least complicated.

11 **(3:07)** **Look and listen. Then ask and answer.**

1 Which one is more beautiful?

3 Which ride is more exciting?

2 Which animal is less frightening?

4 Which one is more important?

12 **Make sentences and say. Do you agree?**

> English is more complicated than Maths.

1 English / complicated / maths

3 cats / intelligent / dogs

5 big snake / frightening

2 a thriller / frightening / a musical

4 sci-fi films / interesting / romances

6 playing video games / important

13 **Ask and answer.**

Who is the most intelligent person in your family?

What is the least expensive thing you've bought?

What is the most horrible film that you've ever seen?

> What is the most interesting thing about space?

14 Look at the pictures. Tell the story.

15  (3:08) Listen and find out. Why is it impossible to rescue Champ? Then act out.

1

Hey Serena, what's wrong?

I **can't** come with you. They know my face.

2

Where are you going?

I'm going to the underground river...

3

Urgh! It's **cold**, **wet** and **horrible**!

This is **disgusting**!

4

Ha! The guards are watching the show.

Now, where's the time machine?

5

I want to go **back** in time. Ten minutes...

NEXT YEAR NEXT WEEK TOMORROW

6

LOOK! There's Champ.

CHAMP! CHAMP! WE'RE HERE!

Ook! Ook!

7

Look at the **guards**, and the **cage**.

It's **impossible**! We can't go to him.

VALUES

 Use your imagination when you are trying to solve a problem.

HOME-SCHOOL LINK

Tell your family what they should do to solve a problem.

 PARENT

> **s– at the beginning of a word**
>
> **s- at the beginning of a word is very common in English. Here are some possibilities:** sm-, st-, sk-, sc-, sp-
>
> It is important to pronounce **es-** and **s-** properly. They sound different in English.

16   **Listen and repeat.**

1 **sm-** → smart, small, smile
2 **st-** → steak, strange, street
3 **sk-** → skeleton, ski, skate
4 **sp-** → space, Spain, sports
5 **sc-** → scary, school, screen

17 **Listen, point and say.**

1 eskimo ≠ skull   2 escape ≠ scary   3 estimate ≠ street

18 **Read and practise with your partner.**

1 An **eskimo** lives in this igloo.
2 They **estimate** very high costs for the new TV programme.
3 This unit is about **space.**
4 We met on the **street** yesterday.
5 The thieves tried to **escape.**
6 I don't like **scary** films.

19 **Read and blend the words with your partner.**

s-		es-
sm → smoke, smell, smooth	**sp** → spot, speak, spring	**es**kimo
st → statue, storm, stripe	**sc** → scar, scheme, scarf	**es**cape
sk → sky, skin, skirt		**es**timate

20   **Listen and repeat.**

SOUNDS FUN!

The **sm**all **st**ars are **sp**arkling across the **sk**y.
The **sp**aceship is moon-**sk**ating but I don't know why!

21 **Read and find the words in the text.**

Distorting mirrors   concave   convex   reflect   distorted image   curved mirror

Have you ever seen a distorting mirror? They are usually in Science museums and amusement parks and make things appear very short and wide or very tall and thin, depending on how the mirror is curved.

Normal mirrors are called 'plane mirrors' and the image they reflect is not distorted. Concave mirrors are curved inwards so we appear taller and thinner. Convex mirrors are curved outwards so we look shorter and wider. It's fun to see how our reflection changes with the different mirrors!

This mirror reflects my real image.

This mirror makes me wider! I look very heavy.

This mirror makes me thinner!

1 **2** **3**

This mirror makes me taller and my legs look longer!

This mirror makes me shorter!

4 **5**

LOOK!

He/she says that …

They say that …

What does the puppet say he looks like in front of each mirror?

In picture 1 he says he looks real.

22 **Ask and answer.**

1 Which mirror makes the puppet short and wide?

2 Which mirror makes the puppet's legs very long?

3 Which mirror reflects the puppet as it is?

4 Do we use concave and convex mirrors in our daily life?

23 **Look at the pictures. Discuss the different uses of these mirrors.**

I think convex traffic mirrors are necessary...

Wider world

five **space** facts!

24 **Read and match.**

1 How is a star born?

2 When did the first man land on the Moon?

3 Who realized that the Earth moves around the sun?

4 Who was the first man in space?

5 Why is Pluto no longer a planet?

a

In 1961, American astronauts Buzz Aldrin and Neil Armstrong were the first men on the Moon. Armstrong said that it was a small step for man, but a giant leap for mankind.

b

Nicholas Copernicus was a very important Polish astronomer who discovered many interesting things. In 1543 his studies showed that the Sun did not move, but the Earth and many other planets rotate around the Sun.

c

Stars are made of gas and dust. Stars form when the universe creates a centre of gravity.

d

In 1930 Pluto was discovered deep in space. Many years later, the International Astronomical Union decided that Pluto wasn't a planet because it doesn't move around the sun.

e

Yuri Gagarin was the first man in space. He was a brave Russian astronaut who completed a dangerous journey to outer space in 1961. He was awarded many medals and high honours.

25 **Ask and answer.**

1 Why did Yuri Gagarin receive many medals and high honours?

2 Why do you think that Nicholas Copernicus was such an important astronomer?

3 How do you think Aldrin and Armstrong felt when they landed on the moon?

26 **Think about what astronomers will discover in the future. Tell your partner.**

PORTFOLIO

Research on planets.

Make a poster about a planet that you find interesting. Use labels, captions, diagrams and notes to show the information.

27 Play the game using space words. Use your notebook. **HAVE FUN!**

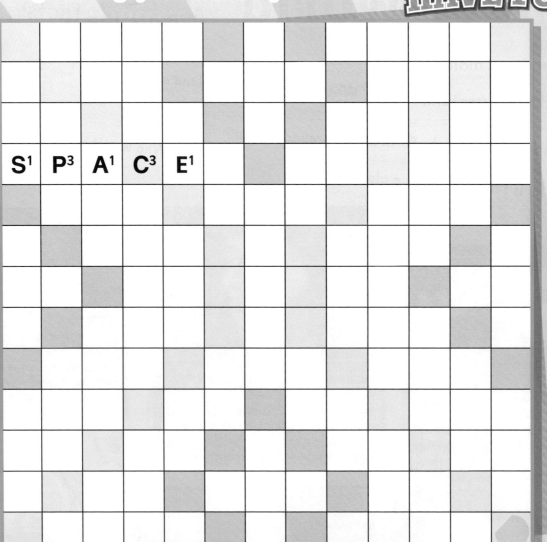

S¹ P³ A¹ C³ E¹

My words	My points
1 space	12
2	
3	
4	
5	
6	
7	
8	
TOTAL	

	A	B	C	D	E	F	G	H	I	J	K	L	M
Points	1	3	3	4	1	5	3	4	1	8	7	3	5

	N	O	P	Q	R	S	T	U	V	W	X	Y	Z
Points	2	1	3	10	2	1	1	1	5	5	10	5	10

28 Play Crazy Day! Say something crazy using _____'d better, should and ought to.

> We'd better look at the stars with a telephone.

green ☐ = letter points ×2

blue ☐ = letter points ×3

Picture Dictionary

AB p.110

29 **Look and say in alphabetical order.**

30 **Read and choose the right word.**

You *(need to / should / must)* have a good night's sleep every night.

They *(should / have / did)* use a telescope, because they may see stars.

There are *(many / few / far)* interesting things to learn about space. I love Astronomy!

31 **Read and ask.**

A

Ask B:

1 Should we use a telescope to see the stars?

2 What should you study to become an astronaut?

3 Should we contact people from other planets?

B

Ask A:

1 Do we need to discover other planets?

2 Should astronauts go back to the moon?

3 Should tourists travel to space?

4 Which planet do you think is the most complicated to travel to?

8 The environment

1 3:14 **Listen and read. What makes Flo sad?**

1

It's the last day of camp. I'm sad.

Come on! Let's clean up!

2

Are you going to help?

Yes, I am. We're going to collect the rubbish.

3

I'm going to switch off the lights in the kitchen.

And I'm going to recycle the bottles.

4

Well, you're all busy ... I'm going to watch!

2 3:15 **Listen and repeat.**

1 recycle paper

2 recycle bottles

3 collect rubbish

4 reuse plastic bags

5 turn off the lights

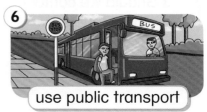

6 use public transport

3 **Ask and answer.**

What does your family do?

What do you do at school?

LOOK!

I'm **going** to recycle paper **because** we need to protect our environment.

He's/She's going to recycle bottles.

We're/They're going to collect rubbish.

Are you going to help? Yes, I am. / No, I'm not.

4 **Read the story again. Talk to your partner. What are they going to do?**

He's going to …

She's going to …

They're going to …

5 3:16 **Listen and match. Then say.**

1

2

3

a

b

c

6 **Look and find. Then say.**

1 five things to turn off

2 four things to recycle

3 three things to clean

7 3:18 **Listen and repeat.**

1
save trees

2
save resources

3
keep the planet clean

4
reduce waste

5
conserve energy

6
reduce pollution

8 3:19 **Listen to the song. What is the singer going to see and hear?** SONG

What's the most beautiful place of all?
Is it the pyramids of Egypt, or is it Angel Falls?
I'm going to find out, going to travel everywhere
To see our wonderful world, see it from the air.

I'm going to fly over the blue rivers and seas.
I'm going to hear the monkeys chatter in the trees.
I'm going to see the highest mountains, covered in snow.
I'm going to the busiest cities, full of lights and roads.

So what's the most beautiful place in the world?
I'm not sure I can say, I really don't know.
The mountains, the oceans, the fields of green,
Let's look after this planet and keep it clean,
Keep it clean, keep it clean.
Let's look after this planet and keep it clean.

9 **Think about what you are going to do to reduce, reuse and recycle. Then tell your partner.**

LOOK!

What **can** you do to help?	**I can** use public transport.

If you **reuse** plastic bags, you**'ll reduce** waste.

10 **Listen and match.**

1 You will reduce pollution

2 You will reduce waste

3 You will conserve energy

4 You will save trees.

5 You will keep the planet clean

6 You will save resources.

a if you use public transport.

b if you recycle paper.

c if you turn off the lights.

d if you reuse plastic bags.

e if you recycle bottles.

f if you collect rubbish.

11 **Read and answer. What do you think will happen?**

1 If you wash your car on the grass …

2 If you pick up the rubbish at school …

3 If you go to school by bus …

4 If you don't have long showers …

12 Look at the pictures. Tell the story.

13 3:22 Listen and find out. How do they rescue Champ? Then act out.

1 GOOD EVENING! I am Zero Zendell, and here is our newest animal – a **chimpanzee**!

The most important thing about chimps is ... they **love** ice cream.

I'm going to give the chimp this ice cream and ...

2

3 Champ does **not** like ice cream!

Quick!

ZERO ZENDELL'S TIME MACHINE

4 Champ!

Wait! Stop! You can't do that!!

Ook!

5 You stole my chimpanzee! Now **I'm** going to **take him home**!

Uurrghh!

6 GOODBYE SERENA! THANK YOU!

GOODBYE MY FRIENDS FROM THE PAST! And good luck!

OOOOOK!!

Save our planet. Learn to save energy and keep the planet clean!

Tell your family about ways to save energy at home.

Suffixes -tion / -sion

Nouns are often made by adding a suffix to a verb. -tion and -sion are suffixes and they are pronounced in a different way.

You add -tion if the verb ends with -t or -e:
act → action, motivate → motivation.

You add -sion if the verb ends with -se, -de or -ert:
revise → revision, decide → decision, convert → conversion

14   **Listen and repeat.**

-tion   -sion

1 invasion / communication 2 motivation / decision 3 investigation/ explosion
4 information / creation 5 pollution / reduction 6 production / conclusion
7 fiction / action

15 **Listen, point and say.**

1 communicate → communication   2 explode → explosion
3 inform → information   4 convert → conversion
5 succeed → succession   6 pollute → pollution
7 decide → decision   8 reduce → reduction

16   **Listen and read. Then repeat.**

1 Communication and information are very important in the 21ˢᵗ century.
2 The reduction of pollution is necessary in our cities.
3 Students need motivation and action in their lessons.
4 Yesterday I watched a science fiction film.
5 This investigation is very interesting.

17 **Read and blend the words with your partner.**

-sion	-ssion	-tion	-ation
convert	proceed	pollute	motivate
explode	succeed	reduce	investigate
decide	recede	act	transport

18   **Listen and repeat.**

There is too much action
in this fiction film production.

19 **Read the text and find the words in the box.**

allergies   ambulance   pollution   sneezing

Allergies

Clean air is very important for your health. If you go to China, you may see a lot of people who cover their mouth with a special mask because of the pollution there. Modern urban life with its cars and factories makes more people suffer from allergies than in the past.

You can also suffer from allergies in the countryside where the air is clean and healthy. This is due to the plants and flowers in the fields.

If you are allergic to something you will probably have symptoms such as sneezing, red eyes and you may find it difficult to breathe. If you have a severe allergic reaction to something you should call an ambulance or go to the doctor's. Some allergies are dangerous and so you should always ask for help if you don't feel well. Allergies are a serious health problem in modern life.

20 **Answer this questionnaire to find out how likely you are to develop an allergy.**

Yes or no?

1	Do you live in a city environment?	**Yes / No**
2	Do you live near a main road?	**Yes / No**
3	Do your parents smoke?	**Yes / No**
4	Do you usually get ill when spring arrives?	**Yes / No**
5	Do you sneeze when you go to the countryside?	**Yes / No**

Answer key

4 or 5 'no' answers It is very unlikely that you have allergies.

2 or 3 'yes' answers You may have some allergy symptoms in the future.

5 'yes' answers Don't worry! Not everyone develops allergies!

21 **Read and say *Yes* or *No*.**

1 If you **live** in a developed country, you **are** more likely to suffer from an allergy.

2 If you **have** an allergy, you **will suffer** from terrible toothache.

3 If you **are** allergic to pollen, you **can't live** in a city.

4 If you **are** allergic to diesel fumes, you **can live** in a city near a main road.

5 If you **have** a severe allergic reaction, **call** an ambulance.

Wider world

What are we doing to our planet?

22 (3:29) **Listen and read. Then match.**

1 Air pollution

Air pollution has many causes. Factories, cars, lorries, and planes burn fuel and send poisonous gases into the air. These make us ill. Then, on some parts of the planet, large areas of forest are burned every year for farming. The smoke goes into the air, too. We need to use cleaner sources of energy, for example solar energy, wind energy, and the natural force of the water in big rivers.

2 Global warming

Have you ever been inside a car parked in the sun? When the windows are closed, it gets hotter and hotter inside the car. The poisonous gases around the Earth are similar to the closed windows in a car. The earth gets hotter and hotter. This is called global warming. Some scientists think this is changing the climate. In some parts of the world it rains a lot; in other parts it doesn't rain for years. This could have an enormous effect on life on Earth. We must stop poisoning the air.

3 Tons of rubbish

Billions of tons of rubbish are produced by humans every year. Cans, plastic bottles and bags are a big problem. They accumulate on land and in rivers, streams, and oceans and kill many sea animals. We must reduce the amount of plastic and metal we use, reuse what we can, and recycle the rest.

a

b

c

COUGH! COUGH!

What causes air pollution?

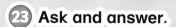

23 **Ask and answer.**

1 What causes air pollution?
2 What is global warming?
3 How can we reduce the amount of waste?
4 What are some cleaner sources of energy?

24 **Think about how we can help our planet. Tell your partner.**

PORTFOLIO

Think and write.

Write a leaflet about alternative sources of energy.

25 Play the game.

1 What are they going to do?

2 You will save trees if …

3

What is he going to do?

4 Why are you going to reuse things?

5 If you are the president of your country, what will you do to protect the environment?

6 You will save some water if you …

7 If we use public transport, …

8 If you recycle bottles, …

9 What is he doing?

ON

OFF

26 Play the chain game!

If I win the lottery, I will buy a house.

If I buy a house, I will have a dog.

If I go to the party, I'll wear a hat.

If I wear a hat, I'll play country music.

27 Play Opposite Day!

If you play a lot, you will pass the test.

If you enjoy the film, you will cry.

Picture Dictionary

AB p.111

28 **Read the sentences.**
Put them in the correct order.

1 Aren't you going to help?
2 OK, you can collect the rubbish at 3 pm. Then I will relax and save my energy!
3 I need a break. If you give me 15 minutes, I'll help you later.
4 Great. I'm going to sit here and watch.
5 I'm going to collect these old newspapers and recycle them.

29 **Read and choose the right word.**

1 If you recycle *(bottles / lights)*, you'll save *(transport / resources)*.
2 If you *(reuse / collect)* rubbish, you'll keep the *(energy / planet)* clean.
3 If you turn *(on / off)* the light, you'll *(conserve / reuse)* energy.
4 If you reuse *(plastic / pollution)* bags, you'll reduce *(water / waste)*.

30 **Read and ask.**

Read to B:

We always recycle at home. If we have some waste paper, we put it in the recycling bin. If we have a lot of rubbish, we always separate food, paper, glass and plastic. Recycling can make a difference to our planet.

Ask B:

1 What do we do if we have waste paper at home?
2 What do we do if we have a lot of rubbish?
3 How can we make a difference to our planet?

Read to A:

If I need to go to the shopping centre, I always catch the bus. I'll walk if I have plenty of time. If you use public transport, you will reduce pollution. Using a bicycle is also a good idea if you can.

Ask A:

1 What do I do if I need to go to the shopping centre?
2 What will I do if I have plenty of time?
3 Why is using a bicycle a good idea?

Goodbye

1 🔘 3:30 **Listen and point.**

The present day

a

c

The future

b

d

ZERO
ZENDELL'S
ZOO

What was your favourite scene in the story? Why?

2 **Ask and answer.**

1 What was your favourite character in the story? Why?
2 What was your favourite song in this book? Can you sing it?
3 Which 'Have Fun' page was the best in this book?

3 Which unit are these pictures from?

a  b  c  d

4 Who said it?

1 'This park is very small.'
2 'I wanted some spaghetti.'
3 '... and it made terrible noises'.
4 'Are you going to help?'

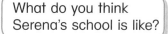
What do you think Serena's school is like?

5 Ask and answer.

1 Do you want to live on Future Island? Why / Why not?
2 What type of boy is Chris?

6 Play the guessing game.

I live on Future Island.
I own a zoo, who am I?

Zero Zendell

7 Look and compare. How are they similar? How are they different?

8 **What are your plans for the year? Tell your partner.**

I'm going to …

I will …

I may / might …

January				
February				
March				
April				
May				
June				
July				
August				
September				
October				
November				
December				

9 **Do you like these professions? Why? Tell your partner.**

I'd like to become a/an … because …

I wouldn't like to be a/an … because …

pilot

policeman/woman

waiter

singer   actor   secretary   tour guide

gardener   inventor   nurse

receptionist   chemist   hairdresser

vet   businessman/business woman   cook   dentist   artist   engineer   firefighter

astronaut

journalist   mechanic   painter   photographer   teacher

footballer

10 Read and guess. Where am I?

a   b   c (HOSPITAL)   d (SCHOOL)

1 ambulances, medicine, cut

2 dictionary, Maths, subject

3 post office, museum, hotel

4 rucksack, tent, torch

Think: What other words could be added to each box?

11 What did you do last weekend? Tell your partner.

first   then   next   last

> First I had breakfast, then I watched TV. Next I played in the park and last I went shopping.

12 Read and say. What are some of your favourite things? What don't you like?

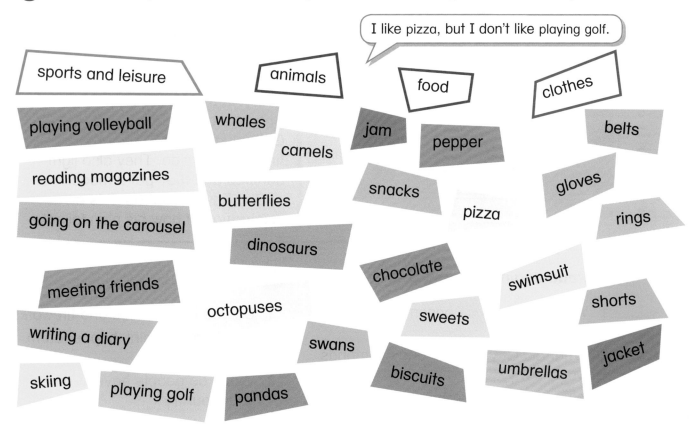

> I like pizza, but I don't like playing golf.

sports and leisure
- playing volleyball
- reading magazines
- going on the carousel
- meeting friends
- writing a diary
- skiing
- playing golf

animals
- whales
- camels
- butterflies
- dinosaurs
- octopuses
- swans
- pandas

food
- jam
- pepper
- snacks
- pizza
- chocolate
- sweets
- biscuits

clothes
- belts
- gloves
- rings
- swimsuit
- shorts
- jacket
- umbrellas

Bonfire Night

1 **Listen and read. What is Bonfire Night about?**

Remember, remember, the fifth of November!

November 5th is an important day in the British calendar. Where does this celebration come from?

In 1603, James I became the new King of England. Not everybody in England liked him.

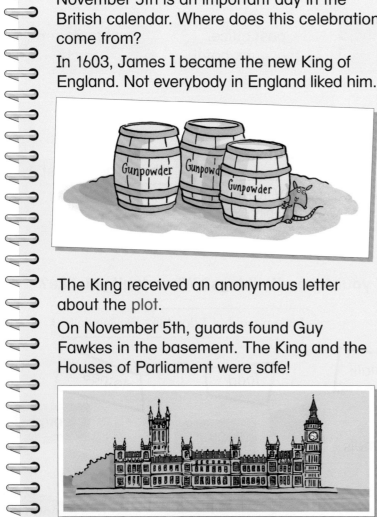

A man called Guy Fawkes and his friends wanted to blow up the Houses of Parliament with the King inside.

Guy and his friends knew about explosives. They wanted to put gunpowder in barrels in the basement of the Houses of Parliament on November the 5th, 1605.

The King received an anonymous letter about the plot.

On November 5th, guards found Guy Fawkes in the basement. The King and the Houses of Parliament were safe!

Every year on the 5th of November, British people remember the Gunpowder Plot. There are fireworks outside. They also light bonfires and they put a model of Guy Fawkes on top. It is a celebration of how his plan failed!

2 **Read again and answer.**

1. When did James I become King of England?
2. What did Guy Fawkes and his friends want? Why?
3. Why do people celebrate Bonfire Night?
4. What do people do on Bonfire Night?

3 **Ask your partner.**

1. Do you like bonfires and fireworks?
2. What do you think happened to Guy Fawkes?
3. When do people have bonfires in your country?

Bonfire Night: Be safe!

4 3:32 **Listen and read.**

Be Safe on Bonfire Night!

Do	Don't
✓ Go to public bonfires. It's safer than having your own bonfire.	✗ Let off fireworks yourself. An adult needs to do this.
✓ Keep pets indoors.	✗ Let off fireworks with your family at a public bonfire. You can give them to the organisers or your family can let them off at home.
✓ Keep fireworks in a metal box.	✗ Light sparklers yourself. An adult should light them. Don't pass them to a younger brother or sister.
✓ Stay with your family. Stay behind the fence.	✗ Hold sparklers without gloves or hold more than one sparkler at a time.
✓ Wear boots. Make sure that your trousers cover the tops of your boots.	✗ Put fireworks in your pocket.
✓ Follow instructions and enjoy your bonfire night!	✗ Relight a firework. It can be dangerous!

Call 999 if there is an emergency

5 **Ask and answer.**

> Why do pets need to stay indoors?

> Why should you wear boots?

6 **Tell your partner. Why do you think that these rules are important?**

7 **Think and say. What other rules could be part of this poster?**

Christmas Crackers

8 **Look and listen. Then read. How do you make a Christmas cracker?**

A man called Thomas Smith invented the Christmas cracker in 1846. A Christmas cracker is a colourful paper tube, twisted at both ends. Christmas crackers are a popular tradition in the United Kingdom.

When you pull from each end of the cracker, it breaks and goes SNAP! Everything inside falls out. A Christmas cracker has a paper hat, a small gift and a joke inside. The price depends on the gift inside.

A traditional way to pull the cracker is with crossed arms. Sometimes people pull crackers in a circle around the Christmas table.

So, how do you make a Christmas cracker?

Christmas cracker

Before you put it together you should save a toilet paper roll from home, write a joke, get some Christmas wrapping paper, some snaps and make a small gift for your friend.

After you collect the materials you should put the joke, the snap and the small gift inside, cover the roll with wrapping paper and tie both ends.

Your Christmas cracker is ready to SNAP! Merry Christmas!

9 **Ask and answer.**

What can you find inside a Christmas cracker?

What do you need to make a Christmas cracker?

What is a Christmas cracker?

10 **Read the text again and find the words. Tell your partner what they mean.**

1 snap
2 crossed arms
3 toilet roll

Christmas: Boxing Day

11 3:35 **Listen and read. Then act out.**

Boxing Day

William: Hello?

Pilar: Hello, William! It's Pilar!

William: Hi, Pilar! Thank you for calling from Spain!

Pilar: You're welcome! Merry Christmas!

William: Merry Christmas to you too! Are you enjoying Boxing Day?

Pilar: Hmm, Boxing Day? What is Boxing Day?

William: Today is the 26th of December. Here in the United Kingdom it is a Bank Holiday. We're having fun!

Pilar: Hmm, interesting … So what is traditional on Boxing Day?

William: It's all about family time. We get together, we play board games and enjoy food. We also watch sports on TV. Later on, we are going out for a walk.

Pilar: That sounds like fun! But why is it called Boxing Day?

William: I think it is called Boxing Day because in the past people used to put food and presents in boxes to help the poor. This happened the day after Christmas. Since then, people have an extra day's holiday after Christmas.

Pilar: Wow, I've learned something new today. Christmas time is fun! I can't wait to get my presents on the 6th of January.

William: Oh, wait! Now you've got to tell me more about that …

12 **Ask and answer.**

> Where do people celebrate Boxing Day? When is it?

> Which traditions are different in your country and the UK?

> Why is it called Boxing Day? What did people use to do?

13 **Read the dialogue and practise with a partner.**

Easter Eggs

  14 Listen and read. What are Easter eggs?

Easter eggs
In the United Kingdom there are many Easter customs with eggs. Eggs mean the start of something new.

Egg decorating
During Easter, people decorate hard-boiled eggs with patterns. The patterns often look like the new, fresh colours of spring.

Egg rolling
On Easter Monday, people have fun doing this sport. People roll hard-boiled eggs down a hill. In some places the winner is the person who rolls the egg the furthest. In some other places the winning egg is the one which survives the most rolls or goes through two pegs.

Egg hunt
Children collect small chocolate eggs that are hidden. They have fun looking for them!

Egg presents
Children receive chocolate eggs as presents. They are covered with colourful silver paper.

15 Ask and answer.

What do eggs mean at Easter?

What is egg rolling?

What is egg decorating?

Which Easter custom do you like the best? Why?

16 Talk to your partner. What do you celebrate during spring?

Making Sticker Easter Eggs

17 🎵 3:37 **Listen and read.**

Materials:
Eggs
Food colouring
Vinegar
Stickers (dots, stars, etc.)
Water
Pan

eggs

food colouring

vinegar

stickers

pan and water

Instructions:

Ask an adult to help you.

Fill the pan ½ to ⅔ full of water and let the water boil.

Add a tablespoon of vinegar.

Add some food colouring until you like the colour!

Put the eggs in the water and let them boil for 15 minutes.

Remove the pan from the heat.

Remove the eggs with a spoon and let them cool and dry.

Put the stickers on the eggs

Your Sticker Easter Eggs are ready!

18 **Read and sort.**

⭐ Remove the pan from the heat.

⭐ Fill the pan ½ to ⅔ full of water and let the water boil.

⭐ Put the stickers on the eggs.

⭐ Add some food colouring until you like the colour!

⭐ Remove the eggs with a spoon and let them cool and dry.

⭐ Put the eggs in the water and let them boil for 15 minutes.

⭐ Add a tablespoon of vinegar.

19 **Ask and answer.**

What materials do you need to make a sticker Easter egg?

What colour will you use for your egg?

What shapes will you stick on your egg?

Why do you think that it's important to let the eggs dry?

20 **Ask a friend. Do you like eggs? Think of a menu for your hard-boiled eggs.**

Wimbledon

21 **Listen and read.**

Every summer, a very traditional tennis event takes place in London during the last week of June and the first week of July. Perhaps you have seen a tennis player from your country playing on the Wimbledon grass. The first championship took place in 1877. Since then, Wimbledon has been part of British summer entertainment.

Some Wimbledon traditions are …

Waiting in a queue. Many people want to enjoy a summer day at Wimbledon. Some people even camp around the grounds!

Naming the players. Married ladies are called Mrs. and single ladies are called Miss. Gentlemen are usually just called by their surnames without any title.

Wearing white. Players have to wear white for their matches.

Eating strawberries with cream. Tennis fans enjoy this delicious dessert while watching the matches.

Don't worry if you don't get tickets! Watching Wimbledon on TV is also very traditional and fun. Game, Set, Match!

22 **Read and answer.**

1 When does Wimbledon take place?
2 Where does Wimbledon take place?
3 What are some traditions at Wimbledon?
4 How old is Wimbledon?

23 **Tell your partner.**

1 Do you know any famous tennis players?
2 What sports do you like?
3 What sporting events are traditional in your country?

A Day at Wimbledon

24   **Listen and read.**

Wimbledon is in the south of London. If you fly to London, there are many different ways to get from the airport to the Wimbledon grounds.

Underground

If you get the underground, the nearest stop to the grounds is Southfields station.

Train

If you go to Waterloo Station, you can get a train to Wimbledon station.

Bus

If you take bus number 493 from Richmond, it will go directly to the grounds.

Taxi

You can always get a taxi to Wimbledon if you are in London.

This is your timetable for the day:

10.30am	The grounds open.
10.30am	The museum and the shops open.
10.30am	The restaurants open for refreshments.
11.00am	The restaurants serve lunch.
1.00pm	Tennis matches start.
8.00pm	The shops, museums and banks close.

Tennis matches end during the evening, depending on daylight and weather conditions.

25 **Read and answer.**

1 What are some means of transport to get to Wimbledon?

2 Where will you need to get off if you get a train from Waterloo?

3 What time do the matches start?

4 What other things can you do in the Wimbledon grounds?

26 **Tell your partner. Imagine you are going to Wimbledon. How can you get there? What would you like to do?**

Extensive reading

Unit 1

1 **Look and say *Yes* or *No*.**

1 Helen is in the desert.
2 Helen's mum is using the map.
3 Helen is with her brother and dad.
4 They have a rucksack for their hike.
5 They found a field with beautiful trees.
6 Helen is excited about the flowers.

2 **Look and read.**

Dear Mrs. Smith,

Greetings from Cairns, Australia!

I'm spending the summer with my family at a campsite. It's so much fun here!

Last Saturday we went on a long hike.

Before we left, we had to get ready. We packed our rucksacks with some food, a torch and a map.

We walked for around 4 hours. We went through the rainforest and we saw amazing rivers and animals.

I used the map key and we found some fields with beautiful tropical flowers.

After our hike, we were very tired! We had a swim in the sea and we made a campfire.

I can't wait to bring my lovely pictures to school!

Yours,

Helen

3 **Read and choose.**

1 Helen is staying at a guest house.	**a** True	**b** False	**c** It doesn't say.
2 Helen isn't having fun.	**a** True	**b** False	**c** It doesn't say.
3 Helen got ready in 10 minutes.	**a** True	**b** False	**c** It doesn't say.
4 Helen and her family were tired after walking for a long time.	**a** True	**b** False	**c** It doesn't say.
5 Mrs. Smith is probably Helen's mum.	**a** True	**b** False	**c** It doesn't say.

4 **Choose the best title for the text.**

a Mrs Smith's summer   **b** Helen's diary   **c** A postcard from Cairns.

5 **Find these words or expressions in the text. Then explain their meaning.**

1 I used the map key   2 I'm spending the summer   3 Yours

Unit 2

1 **Look and say Yes or No.**

1 A dinosaur is flying over a flower.
2 A butterfly is flying over a flower.
3 Butterflies are insects.
4 People can pick flowers.
5 The butterfly is in a park.
6 There are three trees.

2 **Look and read.**

Butterflies are beautiful insects. The first butterflies were on Earth 130 million years ago. During that time, dinosaurs were alive and the first flowers started to grow. Some butterfly fossils from that time have been found.

A few butterflies became extinct but today many different kinds of butterflies can be seen.

Butterflies are found in all types of environments: hot, cold or dry. Some of them live in mountains, but most butterflies live in rainforests. Butterflies are amazing creatures!

3 **Read and choose.**

1 The first butterflies were on Earth a few years ago.
   a True   b False   c It doesn't say.
2 There were dinosaurs on Earth 130 million years ago.
   a True   b False   c It doesn't say.
3 Most butterflies live in mountains.
   a True   b False   c It doesn't say.
4 They have found more than 5,000 butterfly fossils.
   a True   b False   c It doesn't say.
5 Butterflies are amazing creatures.
   a True   b False   c It doesn't say.

4 **Choose the best title for the text.**

   a Insects   b All about butterflies   c The butterfly and the dinosaur.

5 **Find these words or expressions in the text. Then explain their meaning.**

1 environment   2 Earth   3 to grow

Unit 3

1 **Look and say** *Yes* **or** *No*.

1 There are two universities.
2 The boy doesn't look excited.
3 The theatre is offering a tour of the building.
4 There is a post office next to the theatre.
5 The girl is talking on the telephone.
6 There is a factory in front of the theatre.
7 The boy is happy.

2 **Look and read.**

Susie:	Hi, Richard! Do you know that the theatre is offering guided tours?
Richard:	Oh, really? That's great!
Susie:	I'd like to go! Are you doing anything after school?
Richard:	I think I have to post a letter for my mum. I could do that before I go.
Susie:	Excellent! Where shall we meet?
Richard:	What about at the university? I know how to get there.
Susie:	Let's see ... maybe the university is too far away. Why don't we meet at the post office at 4.00?
Richard:	Perfect! See you at 4.00!
Susie:	See you!

3 **Read and choose.**

1 Richard is excited because he loves sending letters.
   a True   **b** False   **c** It doesn't say
2 The guided tour is at the theatre.
   a True   **b** False   **c** It doesn't say
3 Before he goes to the theatre, Richard needs to post a letter for his mum.
   a True   **b** False   **c** It doesn't say
4 Richard and Susie aren't meeting at the university because it's too late.
   a True   **b** False   **c** It doesn't say
5 Richard and Susie are going to spend two hours at the theatre.
   a True   **b** False   **c** It doesn't say

4 **Choose the best title for the text.**

   a The guided tour   **b** The university   **c** Posting letters

5 **Find these words or phrases in the text. Then explain their meaning.**

   1 let's see   **2** excellent!   **3** See you!

Unit 4

1 Look and say *Yes* or *No*.

1 They are having lunch in the school canteen.
2 There are two students and a teacher.
3 He is having a salad.
4 She is having rice and beans.
5 There are knives and forks on the table.
6 There is some salt and pepper on the table.
7 They look excited.

2 Look and read.

Sarah and Jordan were having lunch in the school canteen. Sarah had a good day on Saturday because it was her birthday. 'What did you do at the weekend?' asked Jordan. Sarah was telling Jordan all about the wonderful sweets that she made with her family. 'The sweets were so great', she said as she put some sugar on her salad instead of pepper. Sarah took a bite and made a strange face. 'Something doesn't taste right', she said. At first Jordan didn't know what to say. Then they saw the sugar and laughed. Jordan said, 'perhaps sweet salads are NOT that great'.

3 Read and choose.

1 Sarah and Jordan were in the school canteen.
   a True   b False   c It doesn't say
2 Sarah had a good day on Saturday because she was on holiday.
   a True   b False   c It doesn't say
3 Sarah's neighbour helped her with the sweets.
   a True   b False   c It doesn't say
4 Something didn't taste right because Sarah's salad was sweet.
   a True   b False   c It doesn't say
5 Sarah and Jordan didn't see the sugar.
   a True   b False   c It doesn't say

4 Choose the best title for the text.

   a The sweet salad   b Sarah's birthday   c Rules at the school canteen

5 Find these words or phrases in the text. Then explain their meaning.

1 taste   2 canteen   3 instead of pepper

Unit 5

1 **Look and say _Yes_ or _No_.**

1 They are in a shopping centre.
2 There are 10 children in the picture.
3 There is a harp, tambourine and drums.
4 The date is the 6th of August.
5 The pupils don't like the class.
6 They have some things made of paper on the table.
7 The pupils are playing the instruments.
8 There is a girl who looks happy.

2 **Look and read.**

6 April

Dear diary,

Today I had a great time at school. I had my music class like every Tuesday. Last week Mrs. Parks told us to bring some boxes, bags, toilet rolls and other things from our recycling bins at home. Today she taught us how to make our own instruments! It was so much fun! Guess how we made the instruments! Sergio's guitar was made of paper. He made it with a shoebox. Betty's harp was made of wood. She used an old picture frame. My instrument was drums made of plastic because I brought some old balloons! Now we all want to have a concert with our new instruments!

Yours,

Vicky

3 **Read and choose.**

1 Vicky is writing about her day in her diary.
   a True   **b** False   **c** It doesn't say

2 Vicky was in a factory.
   a True   **b** False   **c** It doesn't say

3 Mrs. Parks is Vicky's sister.
   a True   **b** False   **c** It doesn't say

4 Sergio's guitar is made of paper.
   a True   **b** False   **c** It doesn't say

5 Vicky and her friends want to have a concert.
   a True   **b** False   **c** It doesn't say

4 **Choose the best title for the text.**

   a My music class   **b** My school   **c** Sergio and Betty

5 **Find these words or phrases in the text. Then explain their meaning.**

   1 shoebox   2 concert   3 subject

Unit 6

1 Look and say *Yes* or *No*.

1 The pupils are at the airport.
2 There is a castle behind the train station.
3 They pupils look unhappy.
4 The teacher is counting the number of trains.
5 The pupils are wearing T-shirts and shorts.
6 They have suitcases.
7 It is 4 o'clock.
8 It's a cloudy day.

2 Look and read.

Day 1: Pack light! You won't need a big suitcase. Please meet at the railway station at 1pm. The group will get the 2 o'clock train to Edinburgh. You may want to pack a jacket and an umbrella if the weather is rainy or foggy.

Day 2: Mr. Brown, your guide, will show you the castle. Free time for lunch at 12.30. Free afternoon to visit a museum or to go shopping. Traditional Scottish dancing at 6 pm.

Day 3: Free time in the morning. The hotel might offer other half-day excursions. Meet at the railway station at 3 pm. We will take the 4.30pm train back to Newcastle.

Total price: £200; it includes: train tickets, 2 nights hotel, visit to the castle and Scottish dancing.

3 Read and choose.

1 The group will go to the railway station by bus.
   a True   b False   c It doesn't say
2 Mr. Brown will be the guide.
   a True   b False   c It doesn't say
3 On the second day, they will have a free afternoon to go shopping.
   a True   b False   c It doesn't say
4 On the third day, the hotel might offer half-day excursions.
   a True   b False   c It doesn't say
5 The price does not include 2 nights in a hotel.
   a True   b False   c It doesn't say

4 Choose the best title for the text.

   a Three-day trip to Edinburgh   b My holiday last year   c The castle

5 Find these words or expressions in the text and explain their meaning.

1 the hotel might offer   2 suitcase   3 half-day

Unit 7

1 **Look and say *Yes* or *No*.**

1 They are having a lesson at school.
2 The teacher is looking at the boy with the mask.
3 There are planets, stars and astronauts on the screen.
4 They are learning about space.
5 The astronauts travelled into space in a spaceship.
6 There is a guide who is welcoming everyone.
7 The pupils are not enjoying the planetarium.

2 **Look and read.**

Mary went to the planetarium with her class. A planetarium is a special type of cinema where you can see the sky, the moon, stars and planets. The guide at the planetarium told the class they were going to take a short space trip.
They felt like they were in a real rocket because the stars looked closer and closer. They saw many interesting planets. Some planets had big rings. Some others looked frightening. When Mary went home, she told her mum that she wanted to become an astronaut. The planetarium was great!

3 **Read and choose.**

1 A planetarium is a special type of cinema.
  a True   **b** False   **c** It doesn't say
2 Mary's class felt like they were on a real planet.
  a True   **b** False   **c** It doesn't say
3 Some planets looked frightening.
  a True   **b** False   **c** It doesn't say
4 Mary told her mum that she wanted to become an astronaut.
  a True   **b** False   **c** It doesn't say
5 The planetarium was close to Mary's school.
  a True   **b** False   **c** It doesn't say

4 **Choose the best title for the text.**

  a Stars   **b** The visit to the planetarium   **c** Mary's class

5 **Find these words or phrases in the text. Then explain their meaning.**

1 frightening   2 real   3 closer and closer

Unit 8

① Look and say *Yes* or *No*.

1 The pupils are collecting rubbish.
2 There are 10 pupils in the picture.
3 Everyone is wearing the same t-shirt.
4 They are all members of a music club.
5 There is a girl picking up a plastic bag.
6 The weather is foggy.
7 The field is looking cleaner now.

② Look and read.

Do you like playing in our school playground if there's rubbish everywhere?
What will happen if we don't take care of our plants and trees?
The Green Club needs YOU!
Join us every Monday after school in the gym.
We're going to have fun keeping the field nice and clean.
We're going to do great projects to take care of our environment!
We need you because you are also important!

③ Read and choose.

1 The Green Club needs more people.
  a True   **b** False   **c** It doesn't say
2 The Green Club meets for an hour.
  a True   **b** False   **c** It doesn't say
3 If you join the Green Club, you will be bored.
  a True   **b** False   **c** It doesn't say
4 The Green Club needs you because you are important.
  a True   **b** False   **c** It doesn't say

④ Choose the best title for the text.

  a Join the Green Club!   **b** Our school   **c** Cleaning

⑤ Find these words or phrases in the text. Then explain their meaning.

1 we need you   2 nice   3 join us

Grammar reference

Welcome & Unit 1

See you!
Remember …
We use the expression **see you** for farewells. We can also indicate when we plan on seeing that person.
☺**See you** later! **See you** next week!
☺**See you** in January! , **See you** in half an hour (in + *month or time*)
☺**See you** on Tuesday! (in + *day of the week*)

Questions tags
Remember …
We use question tags to get a confirmation. A question tag is a mini-question after a statement.
☺<u>Statement</u>   <u>Question tag</u>
+ She **is** a nurse,   **isn't** she? **—**
— He **isn't** a pilot,   **is** he? **+**

like + -ing
Remember …
We use the verbs **like**, **love** and **hate** to express likes and dislikes. They can be followed by a noun or a verb in the **-ing** form.
☺I **love** hik**ing**, but I don't **like** sail**ing**.

Be good at + -ing
Remember …
You use the **-ing** form after a preposition.
☺What **are you good** at? I **am good** at play**ing** video games.

Present continuous
Remember …
You can use the present continuous to talk about what you are doing now, at the moment.

+	–	?
I **am** speak**ing**	I '**m not** speak**ing**	**Am** I speak**ing**?
He/She/It **is** speak**ing**	He/She/It **isn't** speak**ing**	**Is** he/she/it speak**ing**?
You/We/They **are** speak**ing**	You/We/They **aren't** speak**ing**	**Are** you/we/they speak**ing**?

☺What **are** you do**ing** John? I'**m** read**ing** a book in my bedroom.

before and after
Remember …
We use **before** to refer to something 'before the moment'. We use simple past and present with **before.**
☺I can't go **before** I **eat** my lunch. I **finished** my homework **before** dinner.
We use **after** to refer to something 'after the moment'. We use the present, the past simple or past perfect with **after.**
☺**After** school I **ride** my bike. I **ate after** I **left** her house.

Unit 2

Describing height and weight

Remember …

We use these questions to ask about height and weight.

☺ **How tall** are you?

☺ **How heavy** is it? or **How much** does it **weigh**?

You can answer these questions by saying:

☺ **It's** 800 kilogrammes.

☺ **I'm** 1.65 metres **tall**.

Comparatives and superlatives

Remember …

We use comparatives to compare two things and superlatives to compare three or more things.

For short adjectives, we add **-er** and **-est** and for long adjectives, we use **more** and **most**.

☺ Otters **are smaller than** seals, and giraffes **are the tallest**.

☺ Butterflies are more beautiful than turtles. Dolphins are the most intelligent.

☺ Swans are heavi**er** than butterflies. Hippos are the heavi**est**.

Simple passive

Remember …

We use simple passive forms to focus on an object or when we don't know the active subject.

☺ Fossils **can be found** under the sea. (*subject + be + past participle of verb*)

☺ Fossils **are studied by** palaeontologists.

Unit 3

Giving directions

Remember …

We use commands to give directions.

☺ **Turn** left.

We use statements to indicate position.

☺ The swimming pool **is** behind the church.

must and should

Remember …

We use **should/shouldn't** to give advice. Note that **mustn't** means that something's not allowed. For no obligation we use **don't have to**.

☺ You **must** respect the rules. (*obligation*)

☺ You **don't have to** wait until the end. (*no obligation*)

☺ You **mustn't** watch this film. (*not allowed*)

Modal verbs: have to, need to, should

Remember …

We use **have (got) to** to express obligation.

We use **should** to give advice.

We use **need to** to express necessity and **needn't** to express lack of necessity.

+	–	?
☺ I **have to** finish my lunch.	I **don't have** to finish my lunch.	Do I **have to** finish my lunch?
☺ She **should** come.	She **shouldn't** come.	**Should** she come?
☺ They **need** to sleep.	They **needn't** sleep.	Do they **need to** sleep?

First conditional (I)

Remember …

We use the first conditional to talk about things that can happen in the future.

☺ **If** I see it, I **will** tell you.

☺ I **will** tell you **if** I see it.

used to

Remember …

We use **used to** for something that happened regularly in the past, but no longer happens.

☺ I **used to** go to Karate classes.

☺ I **didn't use to** like broccoli.

Be careful! **Used to go** is different from 'used to going'. You can use **-ing** when something becomes normal to you.

I'm **used to catching** the bus every day.

Unit 4

Past simple

Remember ...

We use the past simple to talk about things that happened in the past.

For regular verbs (listen, play, practise, study ...) we add –ed (listened, played, practised, studied ...)

☺I cooked stew yesterday.

For irregular verbs we have to learn the past form:

make/made, have/had, come/came, give/gave, see/saw, sing/sang, bring/brought, meet/met, eat/ate, get/got, fall/fell, take/took

☺She ate pizza last Sunday.

The past simple of to be is was/were.

I was, you were, he/she/it was, we were, they were.

make + somebody + adjective

Remember ...

We use the expression make somebody + adjective to show feelings, opinions, likes or dislikes.

☺Playing tennis makes her happy.

☺Will it make you sad if you don't get a present?

past continuous

Remember ...

We use the past continuous to talk about actions that were in progress in the past.

You can use the present continuous to talk about what you are doing now, at the moment.

+	–	?
I was speaking.	I wasn't speaking.	Was I speaking?
He/She/It was speaking.	He/She/It wasn't speaking.	Was he/she/it speaking?
You/We/They were speaking.	You/We/They weren't speaking.	Were you/we/they speaking?

We can use the past continuous in direct and indirect questions but the word order changes.

☺What were you doing yesterday at 7.00? I was reading a book in my bedroom.

☺Can you tell me what you were doing yesterday? I was revising for a test.

Unit 5

Question tags in the past
Remember …
We use question tags to get a confirmation. A question tag is a mini-question after a statement.

Statement	Question tag
+ You wrote it by yourself,	**didn't you?** —
— He didn't make it by himself,	**did he?** **+**
+ You were at the party,	**weren't you?** —
— She wasn't happy to go,	**was she?** **+**

Reflexive pronouns
Remember …
We use **by + reflexive pronouns** to mean alone or without any help.
☺ I learned the poem **by myself**.   ☺ They played by **themselves**.

Present perfect
Remember …
You can use the present perfect to talk about something that happened in the past but is still connected to the present in some way.

+	**—**	**?**
I **have** finished the book.	I **haven't** finished the book.	**Have** you finished the book?
You **have** finished the book.	You **haven't** finished the book.	**Has** she finished the book?
He/she/it **has** finished the book.	He **hasn't** finished the book.	**Has** he finished the book?
We **have** finished the book.	We **haven't** finished the book.	**Have** we finished the book?
They **have** finished the book.	They **haven't** finished the book.	**Have** they finished the book?

☺ I **have** visited my grandmother this week. (*this week=present*)
☺ **Have** you revised for the test? (*you haven't taken the test yet*)

ever, since, for, yet, already
Remember …
We use **already** to indicate that something happened before now.
☺ I have **already** heard that song.
☺ Have you been there **already**?
We use **yet** to indicate that we are expecting something to happen.
☺ I haven't listened to that song **yet**.
We use **since** to indicate how long something has happened from a specific point in the past.
☺ She has been here **since** she was 5.
We use **for** to indicate the duration of time.
☺ They have taken piano lessons **for** two years.

Past simple interrupting past continuous
Remember …
We use the past continuous and the past simple to indicate that a longer action in the past was interrupted.
☺ You **were** revis**ing** when the telephone **rang**.
☺ I walk**ed** through the park while it **was** rain**ing**.
☺ As she **was** rid**ing** her bike, she **saw** a deer.

Unit 6

will

Remember …

We use **will** to make a prediction about the future. We also use **will** when we make a spontaneous decision.

You can use the present continuous to talk about what you are doing now, at the moment.

+	–	?
I/He/She/It/You/We/They **will** …	I/He/She It/You/We/They **won´t** …	**Will** I/she/he/it/you/we/they …?

☺ What **will** you do at the amusement park? **I'll** go on the rollercoaster.

shall

Remember …

We use **shall** to make suggestions.

☺ **Shall** we play tennis in the afternoon?

☺ **Shall** I give you a call when everything's ready?

could

Remember …

We use **could** to make polite requests. **Could** is more polite than **can**.

☺ **Could** you open the door?

We also use **could** to talk about a possibility.

☺ It **could** rain later. Take an umbrella.

We also use **could** to talk about ability in the past.

☺ I **could** run for a long time when I was younger.

may / might

Remember …

We use **may** to suggest that something is possible.

☺ I **may** not have to do it today.

We also use **may** to ask for permission.

☺ **May** I go now?

We use **might** to suggest a small possibility of something.

☺ She **might** go to the party, but she's not sure.

should / ought to / had better / need to

Remember …

We use **should** and **ought to** to give advice.

+	–	?
☺I **should** wash my clothes.	I **shouldn't** wash my clothes	**Should** I wash my clothes?

+	–	
☺I **ought to** wash my clothes.	They **ought not** to go to bed late.	

We also use **had better** to give advice about something that has a possible bad consequence.

+	–
☺You**'d better** slow down!	She**'d better** not eat that meat. It doesn't taste right.

We use **need to** when we think something is necessary. If something is unnecessary we use **needn't** (*need not*).

+	–
☺You **need to** get plenty of sleep.	You **needn't** wash the dishes.

Comparatives and superlatives

Remember …

We use comparatives to compare two things. We use **than** when we are comparing.

We use **more** and **less** when the adjectives have two syllables or more and they don't end in **y**.

☺The red planet is **more** interesting **than** the blue planet.

☺Telescopes are **less** complicated **than** computers.

We use superlatives to compare more than two things. The superlative for less and more is **least** and **most**.

☺This is **the least** famous galaxy.

☺He is **the most** famous astronaut in Spain.

Reported speech

Remember …

We use reported speech to talk about what someone has said.

☺He says, 'The test is difficult.' → He says the test is difficult.

☺She says 'I **am** looking at the stars.' → She says that she **is** looking at the stars.

We often have to change the pronouns.

☺He says '**my** brother doesn't like pizza.' → He says that **his** brother doesn't like pizza.

☺They say '**we** like playing tennis.' → They say **they** like playing tennis.

Unit 8

Going to

Remember ...

We use **going to** to talk about plans in the future. You can also use **going to** to talk about something that is definitely going happen.

☺ She's **going to** sing at the party.

☺ He **isn't going to** drive tonight. The weather isn't good.

First conditional (II)

Remember ...

We can use first conditional sentences with modal verbs and infinitives.

☺ I will take her to the airport if she **can** leave early.

☺ If the pizza is good, **tell** me.

Pearson Education Limited
Edinburgh Gate
Harlow
Essex CM20 2JE
England
and Associated Companies throughout the world.

www.islands.pearson.com

First published 2012
Fifth impression 2016
ISBN: 978-1-4082-9089-7

Set in Longman English 12.5/15pt
Printed in Slovakia by Neografia

Based on the work of Megan Roderick, John Wiltshier and Jose Luis Morales.

Picture Credits
The publisher would like to thank the following for their kind permission to reproduce their photographs:

(Key: b-bottom; c-centre; l-left; r-right; t-top)

Alamy Images: amana images inc 69br, Arcticphoto 49c, Aurora Photos 29 (a), **Alamy Images:** aldegonde le compte 97br, Alex Segre 34 (3), 42 (4), 103bl, amana images inc 59 (3), Arif Iqball 59 (c), Blend Images 98t, British Retail Photography 32 (4), Brother Luck 81, Chris Rout 69 (2), Colin Underhill 34 (2), Corbis Cusp 99t, Craig Lovell / Eagle Visions Photography 58 (jazz), David Sutherland 69 (c), DBURKE 38b, Design Pics Inc. - RM Content 29 (2), Dmitriy Shironosov 61b, Emilio Ereza 39 (2), Emma Wood 100tl, Everyday Images 101 (pan), F1online digitale Bildagentur GmbH 68 (fog), FRANCK CAMHI 97bl, Gabriel Blaj 89, GeoPhotos 32 (8), Haje Jan Kamps 32 (6), i love images 100tr, Ian Canham 34 (1), Image Source 88l, imagebroker 29 (3), incamerastock 32 (2), JoeFox 103br, Johner Images 49tl, Jon Arnold Images Ltd 69 (b), Jon Sparks 19 (c), Juice Images 59 (1), Juniors Bildarchiv 29 (b), Justin Kase zsixz 10 (6), 34 (5), Keith Leighton 28l, Ken Welsh 39 (c), Larry Lilac 10 (4), Lin-Ann Lim 34 (10), Losevsky Pavel 97tl, Mark Boulton 29 (c), 99c, Mark Mercer 34 (7), Mary Evans Picture Library 99b, MBI 51, Mike Booth 91, 103tl, Myrleen Pearson 29 (1), NASA 74b, Neil Tingle 102t, 102c, Olli Geibel 68 (storm), Paul King 42 (1), PhotoAlto 48t, 71, Photocuisine 42 (2), Photoshot Holdings Ltd 18tc, Russell Kord 34 (8), SHOUT 78l, Simon Attrill 19 (b), Stock Connection Distribution 97tr, tbkmedia.de 49cl, Terry Whittaker 18tr, Tetra Images 68 (snow), The Photolibrary Wales 34 (4), 34 (9), Thomas Cockrem 19 (b boy), 69 (3), UpperCut Images 10 (5), WoodyStock 49tc, Yuri Arcurs 60, 78r; **Art Directors and TRIP Photo Library:** Martin Barlow 59 (b), NASA 79 (a), Peter Treanor 39 (a); Corbis: Bettmann 79 (e), Blend Images / Ariel Skelley 64 (5), DIVYAKANT SOLANKI / epa 29 (a), Eye Ubiquitous / David Batterbury 64 (7), Heritage Images 79 (b), Kevin Dodge 39 (1), Monalyn Gracia 78c, Ned Frisk 48b, Ocean 97tc, Sygma / Jacques Haillot 69 (a); **DK Images:** 101 (stickers), 101 (vinegar), Andy Crawford 101 (food colouring); **Fotolia.com:** Alexander Trinitatov 28 (girl), Anton Prado PHOTO 68 (drought), arbaes 32 (9), Duncan Noakes 25bl, Eric Isselée 22 (5), Feng Yu 103tr, galubi 25br, igor 25bc, Irina Ukrainets 101 (eggs), Kasia Bialasiewicz 102b, Les Cunliffe 24 (jungle), Monkey Business 47, NDJ 49c, Norman Pogson 10 (2), olly 10 (1), Peter Baxter 32 (7), Sandra van der Steen 100tc, Silkstock 98c,

stocker1970 38t, WavebreakmediaMicro 10 (7), Yevgenia Gorbulsky 68 (rain), Yuri Arcurs 18 (girl); **Getty Images:** Cultura / Johnny Valley 10 (3), John Arnold / John Cancalosi 28r, Jupiterimages 59 (2), Ron & Patty Thomas / Taxi 84, Stone / Anthony Boccaccio 18tl, The Image Bank / Shannon Fagan 39 (3), UpperCut Images / Zave Smith 19 (c girl); **iStockphoto:** Ana Abejon 92, Cindy Singleton 61 (girl), Dave Bluck 24br, Donna Coleman 11, Eric Isselée 22 (2), Jennifer Byron 42 (girl), John Cowie 21, Morgan Lane Studios 14, Nina Shannon 52, 73, sololos 79 (c), Trent Chambers 88r, Valerii Kaliuzhnyi 22 (1), VikramRaghuvanshi 101 (boy); **NASA:** ESA, and. A. Schaller (for STScI) 79 (d); **Pearson Education Ltd:** Jon Barlow 35 (girl), Jules Selmes 31b, 58 (girl), 100 (girl), Studio 8 18 (boy), 75 (girl), 98b, Trevor Clifford 28 (boy); **Photolibrary.com:** Oxford Scientific (OSF) 24bl; **Rex Features:** 32 (5), Brian Rasic 58 (pop), Courtesy Everett Collection 58 (blues), Jennifer Jacquemart 39 (b), Jim Smeal / BEI 58 (country), Newspix 58 (rock), Patrick Frilet 19 (a), Tony Larkin 59 (a); **Shutterstock.com:** Adisa 42 (7), Africa Studio 64 (1), 70, Alex James Bramwell 22 (9), 75 (2 b), Anan Kaewkhammul 31 (4 left), Anat-oli 24 (3), Andrea Skjold 42 (6), Anne Kitzman 64 (3), Arvind Balaraman 69 (1), Benis Arapovic 64 (8), Bill Kennedy 31 (5 left), Blaj Gabriel 69 (girl), Brett Mulcahy 42 (8), Cardiae 24 (7), Catalin Petolea 61 (boy), 67 (boy), Christopher Elwell 22 (7), Computer Earth 22 (6), 24 (4), Darrin Henry 41 (boy), David Davis 99 (girl), Devi 64 (2), Digital Media Pro 54 (boy), Dmitry Skutin 54 (7), Dmitry Vereshchagin 54 (8), Dusan964 24 (9), Elena Schweitzer 9 (d), 54 (4), elsar 74t, Enshpil 54 (2), Eric Gevaert 24 (sea), 31 (3 left), Eric Isselée 9 (a), 22 (3), 22 (8), 24 (8), Evgeniy Ayupov 24 (5), F. Krause 54 (3), Filip Fuxa 75 (4 b), Fivespots 24 (2), Francois van Heerden 25tl, 31 (2 left), Gallimaufry 31 (6 left), Gelpi 41 (girl), 41b, Godrick 75 (1 b), Goldenangel 75 (2 a), Hodag Media 49cr, iofoto 49b, James Laurie 31 (6 centre), Jason Prince 31 (4 centre), Jerry Zitterman 64 (6), Kletr 24 (1), Kokhanchikov 12 (5), Kurhan 35 (boy), Lalito 54 (6), Loo Joo Pheng 25tc, 31 (2 right), Mark Herreid 12 (1), Martin Anderson 75 (3 b), Matthew Cole 12 (6), Micha Rosenwirth 75 (1 a), Mikhail 54 (5), Miles Away Photography 31 (6 right), Monkey Business Images 42 (9), Naluwan 9 (boy), Nick Biemans 31 (4 right), NREY 22 (4), Orhan Cam 67 (girl), ostill 93, Pandapaw 22 (10), Peter Zurek 32 (3), Pierre-Yves Babelon 31 (1 left), Piotr Zajac 25tr, Prism68 32 (1), RDTMOR 9 (b), Rich Carey 31 (5 centre), Richard Peterson 24 (6), RM 31 (5 right), Robert Ford 64 (4), Robyn Mackenzie 54 (1), Rui Vale de Sousa 45, Senai Aksoy 31 (1 right), SergiyN 100 (boy), takayuki 49tr, Tom Hirtreiter 75 (3 a), Tracy Whiteside 19 (a boy), 58 (boy), Ungor 34 (6), Vaklav 31 (3 right), Veniamin Kraskov 12 (2), Viktar Malyshchyts 9 (c), Zastol`skiy Victor Leonidovich 75 (4 a); **Thinkstock:** istock 42 (3), 42 (5)

All other images © Pearson Education

Every effort has been made to trace the copyright holders and we apologise in advance for any unintentional omissions. We would be pleased to insert the appropriate acknowledgement in any subsequent edition of this publication.